San Jose With Kids

A Family Guide to the Greater San Jose and Santa Clara Valley Area

by

**Dierdre W. Honnold
Kathleen Reimer
Deborah McKim
Brian Bates**

Wordwrights **WI** *International*

*Our thanks to our families
for their patience and support,
and for always going along.*

Printed in the United States of America.

Wordwrights International Publishers
P.O. Box 1941, Carmichael, CA 95609-1941

ISBN 0-9640370-2-5

Illustrations by Katy Hardeay and D.W. Honnold
Design and Typography by Tempel Typographics
Cover design by The Flying Mouse

Library of Congress Catalog Card Number: 95-60696

First edition

WHO WE ARE

Parents, writers, travellers, explorers...

* Dierdre Honnold has been publishing articles on travel and parenting since 1981, and has written two books, <u>Sacramento with Kids</u> and <u>English with Ease</u>. With her two children, she's explored out-of-the-way places on three continents, and even finds time to be a musician and a teacher now and then. She's lived in northern California since 1985.

* Kathleen Reimer, a native of San Mateo, has been writing travel articles about San Jose and other points across the country since 1985. Her two sons have helped her explore beaches, caves, and other out-of-the-way places, providing a kids'-eye view of what's really important while travelling with young adventurers.

* Deborah McKim enjoys exploring the San Jose region with her three children. A long-time resident of San Jose, she loves the challenge of travelling and writing about it — while also working hard at the most important job in the world: being a parent. Touring with older children and a baby has kept her perspective varied enough to produce a guide that parents and teachers can relate to.

* Brian Bates, an instructor at American River College (Sacramento), heads Brian Bates Productions, an Educational Media Company that designs and develops educational software. His kids have helped keep him focussed on the needs of students, and when he's not busy developing media programs, he enjoys travelling, especially through Latin America.

WHY WE WROTE THIS BOOK

Knowing that San Jose is the third largest city in California, we assumed there would already be a guide like this to help us find the neat stuff, the out-of-the-way places, the field trips, the fun. But we couldn't find it — so we wrote it.

Now, instead of spending your time on the phone searching for information, you can go out and have fun. There's lots of it to be had in the San Jose/Santa Clara region. Keep this book handy — in your glove compartment, or near the door by your keys. It'll soon be one of your most-used books!

From the 1777 Pueblo de San Jose de Guadalupe to *our* San Jose, heart of Silicon Valley, this area has been part of California's rich history. Explore that history with your family; enjoy the diversity of a region rich in sports and culture and things to do; discover the pleasures of hundreds of parks and places to get away and be together.

Whether you're here for a visit or here for a lifetime, welcome to San Jose!

Enjoy!

HOW TO USE IT

Children have a knack for seeing the essentials, and that's what we've focussed on in this book. Adults have plenty of guide-books; our criteria in this one was family fun. If kids and their adult friends don't enjoy it, you probably won't find it here.

When exploring with children, the unexpected is sure to happen — so the more prepared we are as parents, the better the experience will be. There are suggestions here and there throughout the book, for those places that require special preparations or precautions. But in general, when travelling or exploring with kids, there's one rule of thumb to remember: you can't be too prepared!

Our own recommendations for a successful day-trip in the San Jose region include packing:

* a map for each child (learning to follow along on these fun excursions can be a lifelong skill they'll thank you for later);
* sun-block and/or hats;
* water bottles for everyone (you never know where the next water fountain will be, and kids enjoy the independence of carrying their own)
* snacks everyone likes (nothing like a bite of something sweet to sweeten those flagging dispositions!)
* things to do in the car
* a compass (to hone another lifelong skill that's lots of fun)
* this book

Have fun exploring!

Also from Wordwrights International:

Sacramento with Kids — a complete guide and resource to the greater Sacramento area for people with children. 256 pages.

English with Ease — an innovative way to understand the English language. <u>More</u> than just grammar. 252 pages.

For ordering information, see back page.

CONTENTS

GETTING AROUND

The Santa Clara County Transportation Agency operates San Jose's public transit system, which is comprised of County Transit Buses, Light Rail, and Historic Trolleys. Individual fares vary. Riders may purchase a Day Pass good for unlimited rides on the bus, light rail or trolley. For route and rate information, call 321-2300.

* County Transit Buses provide bus service throughout the county and connect to other Bay Area systems. Riders should have exact fare when boarding, since drivers do not carry change.

* Light Rail operates on a 20-mile rail line (33 stations) and serves the Great America industrial area of Santa Clara, San Jose Civic Center, downtown San Jose, and the residential areas of South San Jose. Trains run from 4:30 am to 1:30 am weekdays; 5:45 am to 1:30 am, weekends. Free shuttles between Metro Station and San Jose International Airport. Tickets may be purchased from vending machines at light rail stations. You must have proof of payment before boarding.

* Historic trolleys operate on the downtown San Jose 10-block Transit Mall loop, 11am-7pm, Memorial Day through Labor Day, weather permitting. Trolley tickets may be purchased from vending machines at any Transit Mall light rail station by pushing the button marked "historic trolley."

* Other public transportation alternatives: AMTRAK (800) 872-7245; BART: (510) 793-2278 or (510) 441-2278; CalTrain (800) 660-4287; Greyhound Bus Lines: 291-8890.

* San Jose Arena Shuttle Service – 321-2300. Free shuttle service between the San Jose Arena, Light Rail System and selected downtown parking garages for Arena events. Call for route and times.

* Taxicabs: Rates are $1.80 at flagdrop; then an additional $1.80/mile. Passengers hiring taxis at San Jose International Airport, add $2.25 to the flagdrop.

* Kids' Cab is a new taxi service to transport kids to all their activities when Mom and Dad are already over-booked. You register your kids and get them a membership card, which indicates how many pre-paid rides they're entitled to. They must show the card each time to the uniformed, trained driver, who delivers them safely to their destination (in the Cupertino/Saratoga areas). 342-0100

> **The information in this book was accurate at time of printing.**
> **But cities, like people, are always changing; be sure**
> **to call for up-to-date information.**

INTRODUCTION

Welcome to California's third largest city, and also — paradoxically — one of the nation's safest cities. Okay, you say, so it's big and safe; but what's there to do? — the burning question of any parent, caregiver, grandparent, teacher, aunt or anyone who spends time with kids.

The answers to that question surprised even us.

We were amazed to find over 125 parks in the San Jose area alone. Add to that all the regional and state parks, wilderness areas and just plain wide open spaces that invite family fun. And for those of you who manage some time for yourself now and then, there are gardens designed just for strolling and smelling the flowers.

But if your kids are like ours, strolling's not quite their speed — so we were delighted to learn that the Santa Clara Valley has more than enough activities to satisfy even the most unrelenting movers and shakers. Every sport you can think of — and some that we couldn't. Enough performing arts to suit any taste, whether your preference is watching or doing. Museums to challenge any area of expertise. San Jose is decidedly a place for learning.

It's also a place with a strong sense of history. Established November 29, 1777, El Pueblo de San José de Guadalupe was the first town established in New California by the Spanish government. It was also the state's first capital. The chapter on Missions and Adobes will orient you historically and give you a feel for the California of Padre Serra and the time of the Spanish Presidios. At the Peralta Adobe, you can experience that era, and imagine living in those tumultuous times when in one lifetime — Peralta's — four different flags flew over his adobe.

Besides flags, San Jose has gone through many names. After many decades as El Pueblo de San Jose de Guadalupe, the area became known as a purveyor of fresh fruits, especially the prune plum, to the whole country, earning the nickname "The Garden City in the Valley of Heart's Delight."

Specialties change, though, and today the region is known worldwide as Silicon Valley, the home of the microchip. Learn about chips at the Intel Museum — just down the road from Great America, Paramount's theme park, and not far from Mission Santa Clara. You don't need to go far here to find places to go and activities to entice explorers of any age or taste.

So hop on a train or light rail or historic trolley, or load the gang up in the car, toss this book in the glove compartment, and you're ready for fun. On the way, you can treat the kids to your rendition of that old song, "Do You Know the Way to San Jose?." Not only will they soon know the way, you won't be able to keep them away from their favorite spots — all waiting for you to discover.

> **Unless otherwise noted, all addresses in the book are in San Jose, and all telephone numbers are in the 408 area.**

1

Places To Go

A s California's first city, downtown San Jose offers visitors first and foremost an appreciation of its past. When your kids start studying California history in school, be sure to plan a stop at the Plaza de Cesar Chavez (South Market St., between San Fernando and San Carlos Sts.). Besides the fact that it's a great place to have fun, especially when the fountains are on in the summer, a marker there describes the time when San Jose was named California's capital (1850), although the capital was never permanently located here. Across from the plaza, where the Fairmont Hotel now stands, California's first legislature met in a two-story adobe. Prior to admission, however, the capital was moved to Sacramento, where it remained.

Not far north of the Peralta Adobe in St. James Square, on East St. John between North 1st and 3rd, is the Santa Clara County Courthouse (1868). The courthouse was built in anticipation of the day — which never came — when the state capital would once again be San Jose. Across the square is the Carpenter Gothic-style Trinity Episcopal Church (1863), the oldest church still in use in San Jose, San Jose's first federal building (1892) and home of the San Jose Museum of Art, and St. Joseph Cathedral (1877).

But time waits for no city, and San Jose has kept pace with the future while preserving its past. More than $1 billion has been invested in revitalizing the nation's eleventh largest city and California's third — projects like the construction of the San Jose McEnery Convention Center, renovation and addition of numerous downtown hotels, and the San Jose Arena, home of the San Jose Sharks national hockey team.

Wherever your family's focus for fun fits on San Jose's timeline, here are some places where you can start getting to know El Pueblo de San Jose.

First, before you head for one of the following museums in the San Jose area, you should know about **Museum Month**. Usually the first week of April, Museum Month helps you celebrate the rich cultural resources of San Jose's Museums by offering admission discounts, reciprocal memberships, membership discounts and other enticing specials. In the past, the Smithsonian Institution has sponsored programs at participating venues, and there are other programs to look for. The first five museums listed below have all been past participants; check with the museums or the Visitors Bureau for up-to-date information.

☀ American Museum of Quilts & Textiles

766 South 2nd St. Located one block south of I-280, between Margaret and Virginia Sts. Open T-Sat, 10-4, except major holidays. Free.
☀ *971-0323*

This small but unusual museum, located in an adobe-style home on the outskirts of downtown, houses a changing collection of traditional and contemporary quilts from around the world. The patterns and colors of the displayed quilts will entice the kids. Although emphasis is on 20th century pieces, the collection includes fine examples of quilts and coverlets from the 19th century. There is also a small gift shop with items for the quilter, as well as books and handmade items.

☀ Children's Discovery Museum

180 Woz Wy., at the intersection of Woz Way and Auzerais Street (southwest of W. San Carlos St. and Almaden Bd.). Open year-round, T-Sat, 10-5; Sun, 12-5. Adults, $6; Seniors (65+), $5; ages 2-18, $4; under 2, free. ☀ *298-5437*

The Children's Discovery Museum, located along the banks of the Guadalupe River, is as unusual outside as it is inside. You'll know it by its geometric, purple facade. Inside, the museum is a fusion of color, sound and motion as children (and adults) of all ages explore the relationships between the natural and the created worlds.

The museum's main thoroughfare is a "Streets" exhibit that includes a 5/8-scale replica of a city street complete with street lights, parking meters, fire hydrants and traffic signals. Community vehicles range from an ambulance with flashing red light to a fire truck that invites exploration.

Don't miss the "Doodad Dump," where the imagination can run wild as you transform recycled materials into pieces of art, or the "Underground" which is reached via slide.

The Discovery Museum offers on-going drop-in classes throughout the summer. Summer '95 theme: "The Way We Play." Also "Pre-School Days" offered throughout the year.

It's hard to tell who is having more fun at the Discovery Museum, the little kids or the "big" kids.

☀ Egyptian Museum & Planetarium

Rosicrucian Park, 1342 Naglee Av. Located 2 miles west of downtown San Jose at the intersection of Park and Naglee Avs. Best freeway access: I-880 to The Alameda Exit. Open 7 days, 9-5. Adults, $6;

Senior/students w/ID, $4; Ages 7-15, $3.50; under 7, free. Separate admission. Adult, $4; Senior & student w/ID, $3.50; Ages 7-15, $3; under 7, free. ✳ *947-3636*

(SAN JOSE CONVENTION AND VISITORS BUREAU)

The Egyptian Museum and Planetarium has the largest collection of Egyptian artifacts on the West Coast.

The front approach to the museum is a reproduction of the Avenue of Ram sphinxes from the Karnak Temple at Thebes in Upper Egypt. Styled after ancient Egyptian temples, the building houses the largest Egyptian collection on exhibit in the West. A highlight of the museum is a full-scale, walk-in replica of an Egyptian noble's rock-cut tomb, circa 2,000 B.C.

An entire gallery is dedicated to mummification, coffins and sarcophagi. Fascinating mummies of a bull's head, crocodiles and humans are among those displayed. Check out the canopic jars, used to store the subject's internal organs, and other funerary objects. Additional galleries include displays of exquisite jewelry, good luck amulets, and artifacts associated with the cultures of the ancient world.

Check to see what show is playing in the Planetarium, next door.

And the Alexandria Bookstore and Café, on the premises, offers light snacks.

❋ San Jose Museum of Art

110 South Market St. (corner South Market/San Fernando). From Hwy 101 N., take I-280 Exit to Guadalupe Pkwy. Head north to Santa Clara St.; turn right 5 blocks to Market, go 2 blocks to San Fernando to park in one of 3 hourly lots. T-Sat, 10-5; Th: 10-8. Adults, $5; Senior (62+), $3; students w/ID, $3; 6-17 yrs, $3; under 5 free. Free first Thursday of month. ❋ 294-2787

Housed in a former post office built in 1892, the Museum of Art is a family-oriented destination whose purpose is to entertain as well as educate. The permanent collection includes contemporary and American paintings, sculpture, drawings and photographs. Until 2001, the Museum will have on display a selection of masterworks from New York's Whitney Museum of American Art. Concerts, events. Small gift shop. The first Sunday of each month is Family Sunday: Free entrance (excluding entrance to Whitney Exhibit), 11-3. Children must be accompanied by adult. Target Stores offer 1/2-price coupons for the Exhibit.

The San Jose Museum of Art is an innovative center for the contemporary visual arts.

The Museum also has a year-round Art School with many children's classes. All teachers are practicing artists (see Ch.10, Summer Classes).

❋ Tech Museum of Innovation

145 West San Carlos St. T-Sun, 10-5. Adults, $6; Youth, Student, Senior, $4; 5 and under, free. From I-280 take the Guadalupe Parkway N. to Santa Clara Street exit. Right on Santa Clara to Market. Right three blocks to West San Carlos. Paid parking at nearby lots. Limited free parking weekends at River Park Towers (Woz Way & San Carlos). Closest parking at Holiday Inn or Convention Center. ❋ 279-7150

Located within easy walking distance of the Children's Discovery Museum, the Tech Museum of Innovation is dedicated to the exploration of today's technologies. You'll know the museum when you spot "The Imaginative Chip," an audiokinetic sculpture by George Rhodes that is part of the Museum's facade. The Museum features six interactive exhibits areas: Microelectronics, Space Exploration, High Tech Bikes, Robotics, Materials and Biotechnology.

Have you ever wondered how a microchip is made? Or worse yet, tried to explain this to a kid who probably has more knowledge than you do? A visit to the "clean room" will answer everybody's questions. Ever watched the Tour de France and considered how bicycle technology has changed since you were a kid? You can use a Tech computer to design your own bike. And robots — they aren't "futuristic" any longer. Get your picture drawn by a robot, or go microchip-to-toe with a robot to test your game skills against his. Well-versed docents are happy to answer questions.

The rest of the larger attractions in the San Jose area are arranged by alphabetical order.

✸ Alum Rock Park   (See also Ch. 3, Parks)

Take I-280 south until it becomes I-680. Take Alum Rock Av. Exit east (right) 5 miles to park entrance. Open daily from 8 to 1/2 hour after sunset. $3 admission/car. ✸ *259-5477*

Although the park's one-time resort spa is gone, the park's mineral springs remain. Nature walks, picnicking, horseback riding available. Visit the renovated Alum Rock Nature Center, a part of the **Youth Science Institute** (YSI), that focuses on local natural history, hands-on exhibits, and a live animal room with native birds, mammals and reptiles. Separate admission of $.25, child; $.50, adult. ✸ 258-4322

✸ Civic Auditorium Complex/Center for the Performing Arts

244 Almaden Bd., between W. San Carlos St. & Park Av.
✸ *277-3900*

Among its spaces are the Montgomery Theater and the Center for Performing Arts, designed by the Frank Lloyd Wright Foundation.

✸ Intel Museum

2200 Mission College Bd., Santa Clara. The Museum is adjacent to the main lobby of Intel's Robert Noyce building. From Hwy 101, take Great America Parkway exit north to Mission College Bd; turn right to the Robert Noyce Building, on right. Park in visitor/customer spaces. Keep in mind that you're entering the museum through the company

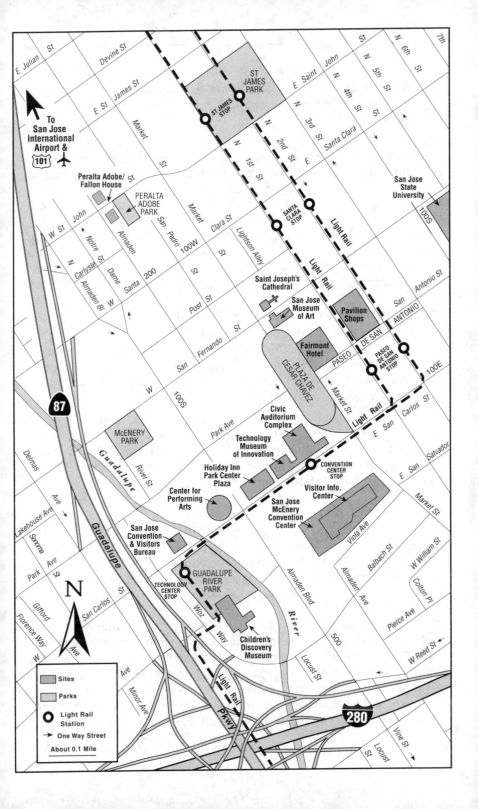

lobby and don't be intimidated by the decidedly formal atmosphere; this place is indeed visitor friendly. Open M-F, 8-5, excluding holidays. Free. ✹ *765-0503*

Intel Corporation is the world's largest manufacturer of semi-conductor chips, which are used to power computers, microwave ovens and traffic lights, among other things. A self-guided tour of the museum describes the world of computer chip manufacturing in a non-technical way that is understandable for those from elementary school age to adult.

See how chips are constructed and used, and learn about key players in the history of the industry. Computers in the back corner of the museum offer programs like "Sim City," "Sim Life," "Digestive System," etc. Changing exhibits mean enjoyable repeat visits.

✹ Japanese Friendship Garden

Located at Kelley Park, 1300 Senter Rd. From Hwy 101, take Story Rd. west to Senter Rd. Turn left to the park. From I-680, take 10th Street south to Story Rd. Take Story Rd. to Senter, to the park. $3 per private vehicle in summer, and on Saturday, Sunday and holidays. Open year-round. Tours available. ✹ *297-0778*

In this large, peaceful garden you can wander past waterfalls, greenery and flowering trees, and admire the numbers of migratory waterfowl that make their home here or drop in seasonally. The kids will be tickled by the Moon and Zigzag Bridges, and the traditional Koi fish found in the pond. Fish food may be purchased on site.

✹ Japantown

The area bounded by Taylor and Empire Streets and N. 4th and N. 6th exemplifies San Jose's Japanese heritage. The one building that is open to the public is the **Japanese-American Museum**, 565 N. Fifth St.; 294-3138. This historical museum, located in the Issei Memorial Building, features photographs of Japanese-Americans who migrated to Santa Clara Valley in 1890.

Although there is no formal tour of the rest of Japantown, you can walk, or drive through the area to imagine what it might have been like. The **Japantown Certified Farmers' Market** is held every Sunday, rain or shine, from 8:30-1, on Jackson St. between 7th & 8th. You'll find a number of Japanese restaurants in the area (several, such as Ginza Cafe, Kazoo and Yokohama, offer tatami seating for a traditional experience) where you can round off your cultural tour with a meal.

Other places of note in Japantown:

* 205 Jackson St. One of the early boarding houses for male Japanese farm-workers.
* 587 N. Sixth St. This woodframe building housed live Japanese theater and was later used to show films.
* 566 N. Fifth St. Wesley United Methodist Church (1941)
* 640 N. Fifth St. San Jose Buddhist Church Betsuin (1937)

❋ Mirassou Winery

3000 Aborn Rd. Open year-round for tastings. ❋ *274-4000*

Fifth generation winery of the Pellier-Mirassou family. Pierre Pellier emigrated from the La Rochelle region of France in 1848 and brought cuttings of varietal stock. He introduced Folle Blanche, Grey Riesling and French Colombard grapes. His oldest daughter married Pierre Mirassou. The champagne operation now is housed in the historic Novitiate Winery in Los Gatos.

See Chapter 6, Festivals and Special Events, for the many special happenings that take place here at the winery.

❋ Municipal Rose Gardens

Naglee and Dana Avenues. One block west of Egyptian Museum. From I-280, go North on Bascom to Naglee. Turn right on Naglee. Open year-round. Free. ❋ *277-5562*

Here's a place where you can stop and smell the roses. In fact, there are over 150 varieties of roses among the 5,000 plantings in the park.

❋ Municipal Stadium (see Ch.5, Sports)

1435 Senter Rd. at E. Alma ❋ *297-1435*

Hundreds of major league players and some Hall of Famers got their start at the Municipal Stadium, also home of the San Jose Giants since 1988.

❋ Paramount's Great America

Great America Pkwy., Santa Clara. From I-880 take Highway 237 to Great America Pkwy. Open mid-March through mid-October, including weekends March-May and all of Easter week; daily June-August, and weekends through mid-October. Call for hours. Ages 3-6, $12.95;

Ages 7-54, $25.95; Senior (55+), $18.95; under 3 free. Parking: $5. Entrance fee includes use of all rides, shows and attractions. Additional charge for concerts. ✳ *988-1776*

Paramount's Great America is a family entertainment center whose thrilling rides, shows, lifesize characters and children's areas are all designed around movie themes and offer fun for all ages. It's an all-day destination, and one where little ones can become easily tired. For a happier visit, avoid weekends and arrive early. Consider multiple-day family pass.

✳ Peralta Adobe & Fallon House

175 W. St. John St. From I-280 North or South take 87 Guadalupe Pkwy north. Exit Santa Clara St. Right on Santa Clara, left on San Pedro, left on W. St. John. From Hwy 101 North or South take I-280 and follow same directions. Open W-Sun, 11-4. Free parking. Adults, $6; Seniors, $5; Children, $3. ✳ *993-8182*

Tours of The Peralta Adobe, the only remaining structure from "El Pueblo de San José de Guadalupe," and the Fallon House offer a look at daily life of the pueblo. Luís Peralta, the adobe's original proprietor, was the supervisor, or Comisionado, of the pueblo's government from 1807 to 1822. During his lifetime, the Spanish, Mexican, Bear and American flags flew over his adobe.

The Fallon House, a showpiece 15-room Victorian home across the street, was built by one-time mayor Thomas Fallon in 1855. It's furnished with period antiques that illustrate daily life in San Jose during the Civil War period. Also on site, The City Store gift shop includes a selection of books on the Valley's history.

✳ Emma Prusch Farm

(see also Ch. 2 Pets, Animals and Wildlife)

647 South King Rd. From I-680, take King Road exit and turn left under the freeway. Right on King Rd. Go 1/2 block and turn right into the driveway. Open daily from 8:30 to 4:30. No admission or parking fee. Dogs on leash okay except near barn/small animal area. Do not feed animals. ✳ *Tel: 27-PARKS*

This 47-acre park, originally an 86-acre dairy farm, gives visitors a chance to learn about San Jose's agricultural history. Enjoy the 10-room Victorian farmhouse/Visitor Center, rare fruit orchard, small animal area, and barn. Year-round special events include gardening/landscaping classes, cultural festivals and seasonal farmer's market.

✳ Raging Waters

From Hwy 101, take Tully Rd. East 1.5 miles and turn left into Lake Cunningham Park. From I-280 or I-680, take Capitol Expressway South to Tully Rd.; turn left on Tully and left into the park. Open on a varying schedule from mid-May to early September. Adults, $18.95; Under 42", $14.95; all guests after 3 p.m., $12.95; Seniors (60+), $9.95; 3 and under: no fee. Parking fee $3. ✳ _270-8000_

Water rides, activity pools, lagoons, video arcade, clothing and gift shops, and daily entertainment make Raging Waters a sun-sational family destination. Public picnic area located just outside front entrance (food must be stored in vehicle). Amenities include free changing rooms, showers and baby changing station. Fee lockers available. Birthday party packages available for 14-and-unders (see Chapter 10, Birthday Party Ideas).

For the younger set there is Wacky Water Works, a jungle gym with interactive water slides, pipes and wheels. Families will enjoy floating together along the Endless River, and speed slides like White Lightning and Rampage will tantalize the more adventurous.

✳ St. Joseph Cathedral

90 S. Market St. ✳ _283-8100_

This restored, multi-domed church, constructed in 1877, has exceptional stained glass and murals. Step inside to see how sunlight transforms them into a wonderland of color. The Cathedral is open during the day.

✳ San Jose Arena

525 W. Santa Clara St. ✳ _800-88ARENA_

This contemporary arena is home of the San Jose Sharks, and venue for numerous special events.

San Jose Arena Shuttle Service ✳ _321-2300_

Complimentary shuttle service serves the San Jose Arena, Light Rail System and selected downtown parking garages, 90 minutes before and 30 minutes after Arena events. Call for latest route and times.

✳ San Jose Flea Market

1590 Berryessa Rd. Open dawn to dusk, W-Sun. Weekday parking, $1; weekend parking, $3. Free admission. From I-680 North, take Berryessa exit, right (west). Go approximately 1 mile to parking lot, on right. ✳ _453-1110_

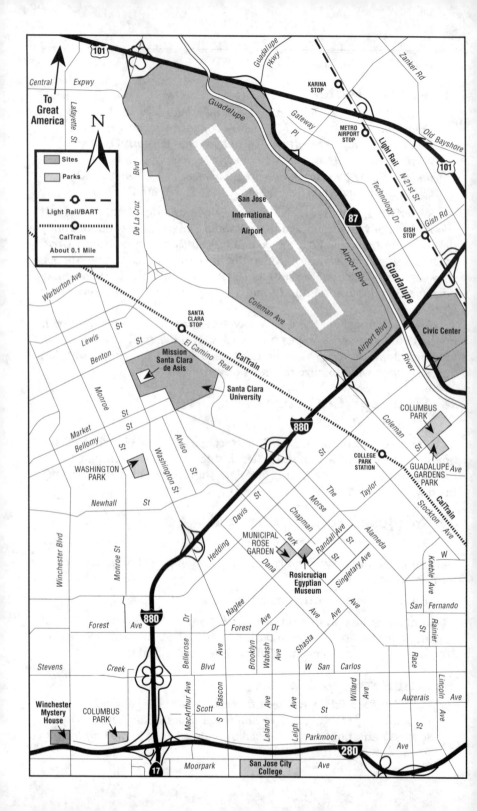

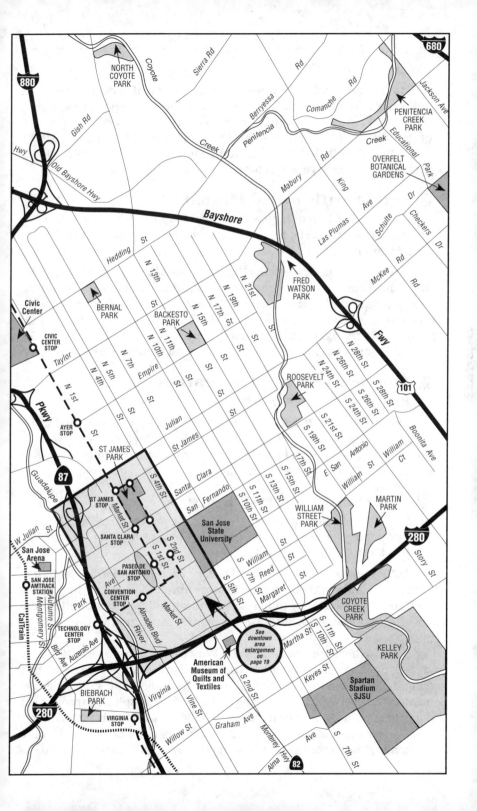

You'll find trinkets, treasures and treats of every variety at California's largest farmers' market, a 120-acre potpourri of sights, sounds and smells. The Flea Market has earned a deserved reputation for its kid-friendly atmosphere that includes carousel and arcade, Kiddie Corral (family-oriented food pavilion), supervised tot lot, and 10 clean, attended restrooms. Pony rides for a fee.

✱ San Jose Historical Museum

1300 Senter Rd. From Highway 101 take Story Rd. exit to the corner of Story & Senter. The Park is located on Senter, between Story Rd. and Phelan Av. Parking fee on weekends. ✱ *292-8188 or 295-8383*

The 156-acre park contains Happy Hollow Park and Zoo, Japanese Friendship Garden and the San Jose Historical Museum that offers a look into 20 replica and restored historical homes and businesses of 19th-century San Jose. This can easily be an all-day family destination. Let the kids romp, share the experience of seeing a variety of animals, many on the rare or endangered species list, and enjoy a bit of history together.

✱ San Jose McEnery Convention Center

150 W. San Carlos St. ✱ *277-3900*

Opened in 1989, the San Jose McEnery Convention Center is considered the cornerstone of downtown San Jose's revitalization. Soaring glass walls, archways and patterned terrazzo floors combine to provide a place of both beauty and function.

✱ Winchester Mystery House

525 S. Winchester Bd. From I-280 take the Stevens Creek Bd. Exit. Open daily except Christmas; tour hours vary by season. ✱ *247-2101*

Aptly named, the Winchester Mystery House (California Registered Historical Landmark No. 868) offers an intriguing journey into Sarah Winchester's obsession with the supernatural. Although speculation continues, the real story behind the mansion appears to have died with its mistress, in 1922.

Sarah Winchester, heiress to the Winchester rifle fortune, was convinced by a spiritual medium that the deaths of her husband and daughter were the result of the loss of life from the Winchester rifle. Her mission, she believed, was to build a home for the spirits, a project she undertook on a 24-hour basis between 1884 and 1922, when she died.

The bizarre Victorian structure she created ("home" would be a misnomer), was reportedly never entered by a guest, only an array of

(SAN JOSE CONVENTION AND VISITORS BUREAU)

The beautiful yet bizarre Winchester Mystery House is filled with oddities.

servants needed to keep the 160-room mansion functioning for its mistress, and, according to more recent observations, a series of ghosts.

Guided tours that follow a maze of halls, stairways and rooms take approximately 1-1/4 hours. Among oddities are a pantry door that opens into a hallway; a window in the floor used to observe kitchen staff, below; a stairway that leads to the ceiling, and another that rises only nine feet yet contains seven turns and 44 steps. These tours are quite a walk; recommended for children over age five.

HISTORIC HOMES AND MUSEUMS

☀ Ardenwood Historic Farm

34600 Ardenwood Bd., Fremont. Take I-880 to Dumbarton Bridge turnoff. Go West on Hwy 84 and take Ardenwood Bd. Exit. Turn right at signal and look for Ardenwood Sign. Open Th-Sun, 10-4. Adults, $6; Seniors $4, Children 4-17, $3.50. Ages 3 & under free. Patterson

House Tour for 6 yrs. or older. Opens early April. ✳ *(510) 791-4196 or 792-0199*

At Ardenwood Historic Farm, part of the East Bay Regional Park District, you can step back into turn-of-the-century farm life. Tours include a visit to the home of George Patterson, who accrued his wealth by farming the surrounding land, a demonstration of farm chores, an explanation of Victorian social graces, and a wagon ride around the 205-acre farm.

✳ Campbell Historical Museum

51 N. Central Av., Campbell. Open T-Sat, 1:30-4:30. Free.
✳ *866-2119*

Changing exhibits contain artifacts typical of the city's agricultural past. Docent-led tours, lectures and special programs.

✳ Cupertino Historical Society & Museum

10185 N. Stelling Rd., Cupertino ✳ *973-1495*

This museum illustrates the city's history through changing historical exhibits, museum tours and a traveling "history trunk" program for schools and community organizations. Open W-Sat, 10-4 and by appointment.

✳ De Saisset Museum

Santa Clara University, 500 El Camino Real, Santa Clara. From Hwy. 101, exit to I-880 south. Take The Alameda exit right to New El Camino Real. The University entrance will be on the left. Free.
✳ *554-7840*

Displays paintings, decorative arts, an early California history collection concerning Mission Santa Clara, and changing exhibits.

✳ Fallon House/Peralta Adobe

(see above, this chapter)

✳ Forbes Mill Regional Museum

75 Church St., Los Gatos. $1 donation. ✳ *395-7375*

This California Historic Landmark, and Los Gatos' first business, was once a flour mill. The museum, located in the mill annex, contains exhibits and photos that depict life in Los Gatos from the 1880s.

✳ Gilroy Historical Museum

Housed in 1910 Carnegie Library, 195 Fifth St., Gilroy. M-F, 9-5; Sat. for special exhibits/tours, by appointment. Free. ✳ *848-0470*

Collection contains over 20,000 objects relating to Gilroy's history.

✳ Harris-Lass Historic Museum

1889 Market St., Santa Clara. From I-880 North, take Washington St. Exit to Market St. Open weekends 10-4. ✳ *249-7905*

Located on the last farm site in the City of Santa Clara, and named for the two families who owned it prior to purchase by city of Santa Clara in 1987. Restored, two-story Italianate-style house, barn, tank house, summer kitchen and chicken coop on nearly one acre.

✳ Harvey-Baker House

238 E. Romie Ln., near Main St., Salinas. From Hwy 101, take Main St. Exit to Romie. Turn left to 238. Open first Sunday of month, 1-4. Free. ✳ *424-7155*

This Victorian-era house was built in 1868 as the home of Salinas' first mayor, Isaac Harvey. It's a living history museum featuring period furnishings, 19th-century fashions, and assorted artifacts.

✳ Hensley Historic District

North of St. James Square

This one-square mile area encompasses the largest collection of original Victorian residences in the South San Francisco Bay Area.

✳ Iron Man Museum

Located in the former Joshua Hendy Iron Works, 401 E. Hendy Av., Sunnyvale ✳ *735-2643*

Exhibits of gold mining equipment and memorabilia from WWI and II, as well as major mechanical and electrical devices manufactured at the site. Open by appointment only. Free.

✳ Lathrop House

627 Hamilton St., Redwood City. Take Hwy 101 to Middlefield Rd. exit. Turn left on Marshall and right on Hamilton. Open T-Th., 11-3. Closed Aug and last two weeks of December. Donations. ✳ *(415) 365-5564*

Built for Benjamin G. Lathrop (first clerk, recorder and assessor of San Mateo County) in 1863. Historic post-Civil War house museum.

✷ Los Altos History House Museum

51 South San Antonio Rd., Los Altos. From Hwy 101 take San Antonio Rd. to the museum. W, 1-5; Sat., 12-4. Free. ✷ 948-9427

This redwood-shingled 1930s farmhouse was designated a local Historic Landmark as well as a California State Point of Historical Interest. Its agricultural exhibits reflect the area's onetime apricot and walnut industries.

✷ Morgan Hill Historical Museum

600 W. Main Ave. Morgan Hill. Open T, Th & Sat, 12-4. Free. ✷ 779-5755

This museum displays a photographic history of the Hiram Morgan Hill family, and photos of early Morgan Hill. Rancho maps, rock and mineral collection of note. Tours of museum and town available.

✷ Museum of American Heritage

275 Alma St., Palo Alto. F-Sun, 11-4. Free. ✷ (415) 321-1004

Old-fashioned doo-hickeys and doodads — electrical and mechanical devices from the past century.

✷ Rengstorff House

Shoreline at Mountain View, Mt. View. Take Hwy 101 to Shoreline. Turn north and follow Shoreline to the end. Donations. Open Sun, T, W, 11-5. Directions/information provided by gatehouse volunteer ranger. ✷ (415) 903-6392

The American Dream can inspire anyone, young or old. Henry Rengstorff, who arrived as a poor German immigrant, lived the Dream, going from poor immigrant to wealthy landowner. This Victorian-Italianate home, built in 1867 for the Rengstorff family, is the oldest home in Mountain View.

✷ San Mateo County Historical Association and Museum

1700 W. Hillsdale Bd., San Mateo. From I-280 take Hwy 92 west to W. Hillsdale Bd. From college entrance, follow blue signs to Bldg. 5, parking lot 3. M-Th, 9:30-4:30; Sun, 12:30-4:30. ✷ (415) 574-6441

The kids will get a kick out of the carriage collection, and the whole family will enjoy learning about the Native Americans, the Ohlone, who live in this area through the turn of the century. Bookstore and extensive research library contains historical photos, texts and research material.

✹ Santa Clara Historic Museum

1509 Warburton Av., Santa Clara. Open most Sundays, 1-5. Free.
✹ *248-ARTS*

The Historic Museum, housed in the Headen-Inman House Cultural Center, features historic artifacts and photographs related to the history of Santa Clara. The Santa Clara Founders and Pioneers Room shows how it was "back then" in the time of the founding families and early pioneers of Santa Clara County.

✹ Saratoga Historical Museum

20450 Saratoga-Los Gatos Rd., Saratoga. Located in 1904-commercial building. Open W-Sun, 1-4. Free. ✹ *867-4311*

Exhibits, which change every three months, emphasize local history and Saratoga's past.

✹ Steinbeck Home (now a restaurant)

132 Central Av., Salinas. From Hwy 101 take Main St. Exit to Central. Turn rt. to 132. ✹ *424-2735*

This two-story Victorian and former childhood home of Pulitzer Prize-winner John Steinbeck is now a restaurant. Its Best Cellar gift-shop is open from 11-3 and has an outside entrance in case you're not interested in a meal.

✹ Sunnyvale Historical Museum

235 E. California Ave., at Murphy Park. T & Th, 12-3:30; Sun, 1-4, and by appointment. ✹ *749-0220*

This museum's displays relate to the local Martin Murphy, Jr. family, area agriculture and include memorabilia from Moffett Field Naval Air Station. Docent-led tours available.

✹ Tait Avenue Museum

#4 Tait Av., Los Gatos. W-Sun, Noon-4. Free. ✹ *395-7375*

This art museum showcases Los Gatos/Bay Area artists. Its natural history displays exhibit specimens of wildlife, flora, fauna, gems, and minerals of Los Gatos region and world. The Los Gatos Museum building was the first permanent firehouse in Los Gatos.

✳ Triton Museum of Art

1505 Warburton Av., Santa Clara ✳ *247-3796*

Major national and international exhibits. Permanent collection of 19th & 20th century American art. Sculpture gardens.

✳ William H. Volck Museum

261 East Beach St., Watsonville, directly across from Watsonville High School. Open T-Th, 11-3. ✳ *722-0305*

William H. Volck developed pesticides that saved the Pajaro Valley apple industry. His home dates from the turn-of-century, and contains an unusual collection of late 19th century and early 20th century costumes.

✳ Woodside Store

Tripp Road & Kings Mountain Road, Woodside. Open T, Th, 10-4; Sat/Sun, 12-4. ✳ *(415) 851-7615*

Despite the little moans and groans, shopping <u>can</u> be fun — especially if you go back in time to do it. This was the first store between San Jose and San Francisco. Built in 1854, it still contains original equipment and furnishings. Gift shop, bookstore.

2
More Good Things To Do

The attractions in this chapter may be somewhat lesser known than those in Chapter 1, and in some cases they may be smaller; but those are about the only differences. Some of these will surely rate high on your family's list of favorites. What we like most about the items here is that in many cases the attractions are unclassifiable. Surprises lurk in the most unusual places. Just like with kids — you never know what to expect!

 ## OFF THE BEATEN PATH

These may not be the first places that come to mind when musing about what to do in the region, but that's exactly what makes them a valuable resource for family fun. Chances are you might even find a family favorite among them...

✳ Allied Arts Guild

75 Arbor Rd. at Cambridge Av., Menlo Park ✳ *(415) 325-3259*

Do your kids hate to accompany you shopping? The beautiful gardens surrounding these shops make errands pleasant, and you can all watch the artisans at work.

✳ Altamont Pass Wind Turbines

On both sides of I-580, between Livermore and Tracy. Take 580 east to Livermore.

The unsuspecting are stunned as they enter "The Valley of the Windmills," where both sides of the highway are awhirr with windmills. Some resemble jet propellers; my favorites resemble the inside loop of an old-fashioned eggbeater.

All the wind turbines you see — the largest wind-fueled power plant in the world — generate energy equivalent to more than 6,000 million kilowatt hours of electricity, enough to meet the needs of about 800,000 California homes for a full year.

Each distinct cluster of these turbines is a privately-owned wind power plant that delivers electrical power to Pacific Gas & Electric (PG&E), who purchases the power at the cost it would otherwise incur in generating the same amount of electricity from fuel-fired plants. Wind power plant developers acquire easement rights from local ranchers, thereby providing additional income to help keep ranching profitable.

More information about wind energy is available by tuning your radio to 530AM while driving through the pass.

✸ American Indian Center of Santa Clara Valley

919 The Alameda, San Jose. Take Guadalupe to Santa Clara St., left under bridge, past Arena, 2nd light on right. Center and Library open T-Fri, 1-6. Call for information concerning children's storytime and Indian dancing. ✸ 971-9622

This resource center and gift shop is owned by American Indians, who sell their crafts here. You can learn about the local native Americans through their exhibits of artifacts, dioramas, photographs, biographies of famous leaders and descriptive histories of significant events. The lovely beadwork can be special-ordered. If you have young children, the Center's program of children's storytime and Indian dancing can be a delightful way to introduce them to Indian lore.

✸ Byxbee Park

Embarcadero Rd., Palo Alto

This park adjacent to the Palo Alto Baylands, once the site of the town dump, has been embellished with sculptures that blend with the landscape, like the chevron pattern of highway dividers that point toward the Palo Alto Airport or the earthen mounds that recall the shell mounds of native Americans who once lived here. It includes observation decks with views over the Bay.

✸ California Antique Aircraft Museum

(See "Transportation," this chapter)

✸ California History Center, De Anza College

21250 Stevens Creek Bd., Cupertino. Open 8:30-Noon, 1-4:30, T-Th, Sept-June. Call for Saturday hours. Free for students/Foundation members; otherwise, small day-use fee. ✸ 864-8712

This reference library is dedicated to understanding the past by creating, collecting, preserving and offering the public materials used to reconstruct history. About 10,000 photos, 5,000 slides from Native American subjects to modern scenes from Santa Clara County, and others, among other maps, prints and artifacts. If you're interested in California history, this is a great place to head.

✸ Casa De Fruta

6680 Pacheco Pass Hwy, Hollister. 13 miles east of Gilroy (off Hwy 101) on Hwy 152. Free. ✸ 637-7775

Begun as series of cherry stands, today this is a 24-hour restaurant, fruit stand, deli and Country Store. Saturday evening/Sunday afternoon barbecue and country music. Animal preserve features deer, buffalo and peacocks. Narrow gauge train travels through the property.

✳ Center For Beethoven Studies and Museum

San Jose State University, One Washington Square, on the 6th floor of the Wahlquist Library North. 1-5, M-F. ✳ 924-4590

This is the only institution in North America devoted solely to the life, works and accomplishments of Ludwig van Beethoven. It includes a collection of 75 first editions of his music, several original manuscripts, a replica of a fortepiano from Beethoven's era, more than 2,000 books and other memorabilia. Instead of tracking down this European composer and his history at his home in Germany, your young musicians can absorb some of the grandeur of who he was and what he did without leaving San Jose. Quite a rare opportunity for music-lovers!

✳ College of San Mateo Historical Museum

1700 West Hillsdale Bd. From Hwy 92 take W. Hillsdale Bd. exit to campus. Once on campus, signs point the way. M-Th, 9:30-4:30; Sun 12:30-4:30. Free. ✳ (415) 574-6441

Exhibits depict Peninsula history from Ohlone Indians to turn-of-the-century. Bookstore and research library. Kids especially love the carriage collection.

✳ Felton Covered Bridge

Located on Covered Bridge Road, off Graham Hill Rd. (which goes off Hwy 9) in Felton. Free.

This State Historical Landmark is one of a handful of California's covered bridges. Built in 1892, it's believed to be the tallest covered bridge of its kind in the country. Park the car and walk the bridge, which is open to foot traffic only.

✳ First Radio Broadcasting Site

First and San Fernando Sts.

The first radio station in the world was erected here in 1909 by Charles Herrold. Known as KQW, it is now KCBS in San Francisco.

✳ Montgomery Hill

Evergreen Valley College at Yerba Buena and Villa Vista Roads, San Jose.

Professor John J. Montgomery of Santa Clara College performed 55 successful glider flights from nearby "Montgomery Hill" to demonstrate aerodynamic developments he made following the flight of the world's first successful heavier-than-air aircraft.

✳ Mystery Spot

1953 Branciforte Dr., Santa Cruz. Located 3 miles north of downtown. From Hwy 1 north, take Water Street; cross Ocean two blocks to Market St. Continue 1.5 miles; you'll see signs. At this point, according to Mystery Spot personnel, "you've solved your first mystery!" Open daily 9:30-4:30. Gift shop. Park free. $4 adults; $2, 5-11. Not recommended for under 5. ✳ *423-8897*

This is a place that defies description as much as it does gravity. Watch balls roll uphill and your companions tilt at unusual angles while guides try to make sense of all of this for you.

✳ San Jose Buddhist Church Betsuin

640 N. Fifth St. ✳ *293-9292*

This was the fifth Buddhist church in the U.S. to receive the title of Betsuin, a title of distinction. Its pagoda-like facade and large, sloping brown-tiled roof are visible from the street. A gate-enclosed formal garden stands at the right of the church, with a fishpond and a tortoise-shaped stone island (symbolizing long life). Pine trees, bamboo and palms share the garden space with stone lanterns and small, decorative bridges, making it a calm, peaceful place.

✳ San Jose State University

One Washington Square ✳ *924-1000*

Introduce your kids to one of our finer traditions: take them on a tour of California's oldest public institution of higher learning. This is a four-year public university that has many theater performances, literary readings and athletic events open to the public.

✳ Stanford University

Building 170, Palo Alto. Call for tour schedule and fees. ✳ *(415) 723-2560*

Guided tour of the campus features Romanesque architecture and beautiful Memorial Church. Hoover Tower Observation Platform offers a panoramic view of the university/Bay Area. Call to confirm schedule. Don't miss the Rodin Sculpture Garden and Stanford Art Museum, Serra

St. near Hoover Tower (415) 723-4177. T-F, 10-5; Sat-Sun, 1-5. Tours on Th; 12:15, Sun, 2pm.

✳ State Capital Marker

Fairmont Plaza, between the Museum of Art and the Fairmont Hotel.

Look down as you stand in the "Circle of Palms" here, and see the plaque that contains the historic seal, marking the place where the Capitol Building once stood. San Jose was — briefly — the first state capital in 1850. But accommodations for the statesmen here were too uncomfortable in this new frontier city, and the capital was soon moved, beginning its trek as perhaps the most well-travelled capital in history! As an alternative to San Jose, General Vallejo offered his land to the State for that purpose, but visitors had to stay on a steamer moored at the wharf, which didn't set well on many of the political stomachs. Next the Capital hopped to Sacramento, after which it moved back to Vallejo and then on to Benicia. In 1854, it moved permanently back to Sacramento, where it has remained ever since.

✳ Villa Montalvo

15400 Montalvo Rd., Saratoga (see Ch.3, Parks). Take Hwy 17 to Rt. 9/Saratoga Av. Follow west to Montalvo Rd. Arboretum open 8-5, M-F, 9-5, Sat-Sun. Gallery: 1-4, Th-F, 11-4, Sat-Sun. Free.
✳ 741-3421

Mediterranean villa and home of one-time Senator James Phelan. Arboretum, art gallery, gardens and nature trails. Tours available; call ahead for schedule.

PLANETARIUMS & OBSERVATORIES

✳ Egyptian Museum & Planetarium (see Chapter 1)

✳ Minolta Planetarium (De Anza College, Cupertino) 21250

Stevens Creek Bl, Cupertino ✳ 864-8814

This is the second largest facility of its kind in northern California. It features family astronomy evenings ($4 adult, $3 kids), educational programs, guest lectures, laser shows and a gift shop. Details on laser shows: 864-5791; other details: 864-8814.

✳ Lick Observatory, *University of California, Box 85, Mt. Hamilton.*

From Alum Rock Rd., turn rt. on Mt. Hamilton and take the road to the top. Approximate time from San Jose, one hour. Closed major holidays;

sometimes closed due to snow. Wheelchair accessible. Open M-F, 12:30-5; Sat-Sun, 10-5.

Guided tours of 36" refractor and 120" reflector telescopes daily, each 1/2 hour until 4:30. Free.

❋ Santa Clara University Planetarium, *500 El Camino Real, Santa Clara* ❋ *554-5285 or 4314*

Open to the public on a limited basis; call first.

❋ Fremont Peak SP *(see Chapter 3, State Parks). Take Hwy 101 S to Rt. 156. Turn rt. at entrance to Fremont Peak State Park. (Observatory is behind ranger residence.) Park fee.* ❋ *623-4526*

From sunset on there's something to see, but the best viewing is close to midnight. Many take sleeping bags and camp out (see Chapter 7, Day Trips, San Jose/Salinas/Santa Cruz for more details).

OUTDOOR/FARMERS' MARKETS and PICK-YOUR-OWN PRODUCE

For a fresh-from-the-farm culinary experience, head to one of the area's numerous outdoor California Certified Farmers Markets — or even better, pick it yourself.

California Certified Farmers Markets

❋ Capital Flea Market

Capital Expressway and Monterey Highway. Th, 7am-5:30pm, Sat-Sun, 6am-5:30pm, year round ❋ *225-5800*

One of the area's largest Farmers Markets. You'll find a huge selection and it's open all day. Allow enough time to shop through the hundreds of booths, which offer a variety of new merchandise as well as the typical flea market items.

❋ Gilroy

Downtown, 5th Street between Monterey and Eigleberry Streets. Th, 3pm-7pm, June through October ❋ *842-6964*

A delightful outdoor market with all of the fresh produce you could want from the surrounding farms. You can also get fresh baked goods, and from time to time, arts and crafts.

✳ JapanTown

8th and Jackson Streets, downtown San Jose. Sun, 8:30am-1pm, year round ✳ *298-4303*

This is a slightly different type of farmers' market. Besides all the usuals, you'll also find a wide array of popular oriental veggies that you may not be able to name, much less know what to do with. Talk with the proprietors; they're happy to instruct or explain. Maybe you can broaden your culinary expertise and try some experiments today.

You might want to combine a trip to the market with a tour of JapanTown; see Chapter 1, JapanTown, for details.

✳ Los Altos

Loyola Corners, Bank of America Parking Lot, Junction of Fremont Avenue, Miramonte Street and Foothill Expressway. Sat, 8:30am-noon, May through November ✳ *(415) 949-0773*

A sumptuous selection of fresh produce. Special events at the opening and closing of the season.

✳ Morgan Hill

Downtown, 91 East 4th Street at Depot Road. Sat, 8:00am-noon, June through November ✳ *779-5130 or 779-6798*

You'll find a bit of everything here; fruit, vegetables, some arts and crafts and even face painting for the kids.

✳ Mountain View

Castro and Villa Streets. 9am-1pm, year round ✳ *(800) 806-3276*

You're encouraged to sample the goods as you walk about this open market. They even offer comparison tasting with some of the main crops from different farms, like apples, melons, tomatoes or peaches. Comments are welcome. Special promotions at the beginning of the high season (May) and the Harvest Festival (October). Call for exact dates.

✳ San Jose Downtown

The Pavilion, South First and Fernando Streets; Th, 10am-2pm ✳ *800/949-FARM*

Located in the heart of the downtown area, this open-air market offers produce, flowers, baked goods and more. Open from Late May to Thanksgiving. Free one hour parking at the Pavilion, some metered parking on side streets.

☀ San Jose Town & Country

Across from Valley Fair Shopping Center, in the Town & Country shopping center, Winchester Boulevard & Stevens Creek. F, 10am-2pm (year round); Sun, 10am-2pm (June to Thanksgiving) ☀ (800) 949-FARM

This year-round market is a popular place to find a variety of fresh produce, baked goods and flowers. Come early, since merchants head for home when they run out of produce. July is "Certified Farmers Market Month," when you'll find special promotions such as "Grill Crazy," "Melon Mania" and others.

☀ Pick-Your-Own Produce

☀ Coastways Ranch

Highway 1, 20 miles north of Santa Cruz ☀ (415) 879-0414

Open daily during the months of June and July for olallieberries, October for pumpkins and Indian corn, November and December for kiwis and Christmas Trees.

☀ Valencia Ranch

2760 Valencia Road, Aptos ☀ 684-0400

They specialize in pumpkins, so their high season is September through October.

☀ Emile Agaccio Inc.

4 Casserly Road, Watsonville (corner of Hwy 152 and Casserly) ☀ 728-2009

Strawberries during April and May, and raspberries and olallies during June and July.

☀ Gizdich Ranch

Lakeview and Carlton Roads, Watsonville ☀ 722-1056

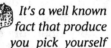

It's a well known fact that produce you pick yourself always tastes better than what you buy at the store! But picking your own can be hard work, especially if it involves stooping over (hard on the back if you're not used to it) in the hot sun. Be sure the kids know what to expect, and — maybe even more important — how to behave: bring hats, wear clothing you won't worry about if it gets stained or torn, and be careful not to walk on what you're not picking (they can't sell it if you've squashed it). And they generally don't mind if you take a taste to see if you like it, but the rule of thumb when on someone else's farm is: don't eat it until after you've bought it.

Strawberries and olallieberries in May/June, raspberries and boysenberries in July. You can stop by their other location (just across the street), 55 Peckham Road, and enjoy a fresh-baked pie and a delicious apple slush. They also have a gift shop and an antique store.

Gandrup Farm

248 Peckham Road, Watsonville ✳ *722-1324*

You can pick fresh flowers, string beans, cucumbers, dill, garlic, apples and tomatoes. Open Tuesday through Sunday from July through September, 9am to 5pm.

LIBRARIES AND BOOKSTORES

San Jose is a culturally diverse community, and that diversity shines through in the programming available through San Jose Public Libraries. Story Hours are occasionally offered in Chinese, Farsi and Spanish, and the Biblioteca Latino-Americana, one of the branch libraries, has a comprehensive collection of Spanish texts.

All branches offer pre-school story time for ages 3-5. Beginning in January, 1996 they'll also offer an after school program for elementary school children. There are special programs throughout the year, such as a "Readathon" in recognition of Black History Month, special programs for National Library Week in April and a themed summer reading club. The theme for 1995 is "Mysteries."

The highly-successful "Grandparents and Books" program pairs grandparents with individuals for one-on-one reading time. Check with branch library for particulars.

Becky Stevens, Senior Librarian, Youth Services, oversees children's services at Martin Luther King Main Library (408) 277-4874 or 4875.

San Jose Branch Libraries (call to confirm hours and services):
Main, 180 W. San Carlos St. 277-4846
Almaden 6455 Camden Av. 268-7600
Alviso 1060 Taylor St. 263-3626
Berryessa 3311 Noble Av. 272-3554
Biblioteca Latino-Americana 690 Locust St. 294-1237

Bookmobile 277-4846
Calabazas 1230 Blaney Av. 996-1535
Cambrian 1780 Hillsdale Av. 269-5062
E. San Jose Carnegie 1102 E. Santa Clara St. 998-2069
Educational Park 1770 Educational Park Dr. 272-3662
Empire 491 E. Empire St. 286-5627
Evergreen 2635 Aborn Rd. 238-4433
Hillview 2255 Ocala Av. 272-3100
Pearl Avenue 4270 Pearl Av. 265-7833
Rosegarden 1580 Naglee Av. 998-1511
Santa Teresa 290 International Circle 281-1878
Seven Trees 3597 Cas Dr. 629-4535
West Valley 1243 San Tomas Aquino Rd. 244-4747
Willow Glen 1157 Minnesota Av. 998-2022

Libraries-Outlying Areas:

Los Gatos Public Library, 110 E. Main St. 354-6891

Mountain View Public Library, 585 Franklin St. (415) 903-6887

Palo Alto Libraries:
Main, 1213 Newell Rd. (415) 329-2664
Children's, 1276 Harriet (415) 329-234
College Terrace, 2300 Wellesley (415) 329-2298
Downtown, 270 Forest Av. (415) 329-2586
Mitchell Park, 3700 Middlefield Rd. (415) 329-2586
Terman Park, 661 Arastradero (415) 329-2606

Salinas Public Library:
Steinbeck Library, 110 W. San Luis St., near Capitol St., Salinas 758-7311.
From Hwy 101, take Main St. to Central; turn left to Capitol and take Capitol to W. San Luis. Call for hours.
This public library houses a large collection of Steinbeck's books including several first editions, and personal correspondence. Special tours of the John Steinbeck Archives by reservation: 758-7314.

Santa Clara City Libraries:
Central, 2635 Homestead Rd. 984-3097
Mission, 1098 Lexington 984-2022

Santa Clara County Libraries:
Administration: 1095 N. Seventh St., San Jose 293-2326
Alum Rock, 75 S. White Rd. 251-1280
Campbell, 77 Harrison Av. 378-8122
Cupertino: 10400 Torre Av. 253-6212

Gilroy, 7387 Rosanna St. 842-8207

Los Altos:

Main, 13 S. San Antonio Rd. (415) 948-7683

Woodland, 1975 Grant Rd. (415) 969-6030

Milpitas, 40 N. Milpitas Bd. 262-1171

Morgan Hill, 17575 Peak Av. 779-3196

Saratoga, 13650 Saratoga Av. 867-6126

Sunnyvale Public Library, 665 W. Olive Ave. 730-7300

Bookstores

The San Jose area is filled with bookstores that offer broad selections of childrens' literature. The giants, of course, are well-known: **B. Dalton Bookseller**, Eastridge Mall 270-1070; **Barnes and Noble**, 3600 Stevens Creek Bd. 984-3495; **Tower Books/ Records**, San Jose 363-5400, Mt. View (415) 941-7300, Campbell (408) 371-5400, and San Mateo (415) 570-7444. These bigger stores don't necessarily offer special children's programs, but they have a wider selection in general, and if they don't have it in stock, they can get it, usually pretty fast.

If you prefer a smaller, more personal approach to book buying or browsing, you might want to try the following stores. They're all just a little different in some way.

A Clean Well-Lighted Place For Books, 21269 Stevens Creek Bd. 255-7600 (across from De Anza College, Cupertino) has a

 If you've never thought of bookstores as places to have fun, think again. In the Yellow Pages you'll find many listings under Book Dealers-Retail. Here are some of the ways your little readers can have fun while developing a worthwhile life-long habit.

* Storytelling Hour
* Craft Time or other children's activities
* Author's visits
* Character visits. Kids can meet the characters they read about.
* Parenting education
* Field trips

And don't forget to check college and university bookstores (listed in Chapter 10, Colleges & Universities). They often have children's literature, day care, and children's events.

once-a-month storyteller and kid-friendly reading area.

Kepler's, 1010 El Camino Real, Menlo Park (415) 324-4321, caters to kids by encouraging them to read, with their kid-sized chairs and space to roam. Parents might enjoy the extensive international newspaper/ magazine area.

Secret Staircase, 2223 Broadway, Redwood City (415) 366-1222 has a large selection of new and used children's books and offers Saturday story hours, and special events.

Sleepy Dragon Book Bistro 2222 E. Cliff Dr., Santa Cruz 476-9136 (at the Santa Cruz Yacht Harbor) specializes in marine, nautical, outdoor, travel and children's books. Owner Pam Rosengard encourages kids to come in, read, do homework, and buy books. Occasional storytelling, harbor talks and lectures by marine science experts. A good spot for budding marine biologists to browse, while Mom or Dad buy pastries, coffee, tea or juices.

Giant Steps Childrens Books & Toys, 39199 Farwell Dr., Fremont (510) 793-1977, offers summer story hour, concerts, author visits and occasional parties based on book characters.

Kaleidoscope, 1820-41st Av., Capitola 475-0120 is a resource store for parents and teachers. At annual "Play Day in May," families are invited to meet with product representatives to test all of their products. Evening parent education programs.

If you have a youngster with an interest in flying, stop in at **The Airport Shop,** 2635 Cunningham, San Jose 923-2625 to peruse the more than 2000 aviation titles and aeronautical charts.

When in San Mateo, stop by at **Book Caravan,** 168 W., 25th Av. (415) 341-3616, open M-Sat, 11-5:30. Owner Clara Shameson, a retired teacher, has filled her shop not only with books, but hand puppets of endangered animals, and musical instruments. Good selection of multicultural books, and books on tape. Story time 2nd, 4th Saturday, 10:30-11:30; 25% off on all purchases made during story time.

Search no more for that foreign language book (for kids or adults). **Multilingual Books & Tapes** (800) 218-2737 may have the answer. This mail order house will research, and hopefully deliver your requested book in 5-7 working days. Specializations: books in Spanish, ESL materials, and out-of-print books. Books may be requested by title or subject matter.

And although it's neither a bookstore nor a library, the **American Indian Center of Santa Clara Valley,** 919 The Alameda (971-9622), offers a program of children's storytime and Indian dancing. For details on the Center, see the beginning of this chapter.

TOURS OF THE WORKING WORLD

The tools of the trade can be exciting things, no matter what the trade. Machines that bang, whir, smash, crush, roll, clang, roar — what could be more fascinating to a kid? Finding out how things are made is a source of amazement for kids of all ages, and there are lots of factories, companies or other places of business that are happy to welcome children in the greater Santa Clara Valley region. Some have minimum age limits; some have minimum group numbers; call first.

✳ Browning Ferris Industries

The Recyclery, 1601 Dixon Landing Rd., Milpitas. From I-880 North/ South exit Dixon Landing Rd., west. Follow the road, or the garbage trucks, to the site. Self-guided tours after 2 p.m., M-Sat. Guided tours for 10 or more. Open M-Sat, 7:30-3:30. Suitable for pre-school to adult. Free. ✳ 262-1401

California's premier integrated solid waste facility combines collection and safe disposal of waste with modern recycling techniques. Watch the recycling process from the observation area, and visit the education center, where you can learn more about our interdependency with our planet's delicate balances.

✳ Cargill Salt

7220 Central Av., Newark. After July 1st, ✳ (510) 790-8600

Cargill offers a "Share the Harvest" fundraiser each Fall. This is the only time the facility is open to the public. Participants bring packaged goods which are matched at $1/lb. by Cargill and donated to local service agencies. Call for details.

Cargill is the only salt producer in the San Francisco Bay Area, and the largest sea salt producer in the US. At the outdoor museum, you can see the Archimedes screws and wind-powered mechanisms still in use, and see the company's own railroad that transports salt from the crystalizer beds. An unusual but fascinating tour.

✳ Desert Theatre

17 Behler Rd., Watsonville; open 10-4 T-Sun ✳ 728-5513

Call ahead for a Nursery Tour, and learn all about exotic cacti and succulents and their special needs and environments. After the tour, you can wander through their beautifully landscaped gardens, and perhaps take home a sample.

☀ Goldsmith Seeds, Inc.

2280 Hecker Pass Hway, Gilroy. Half mile past Santa Teresa Rd. signal, on left. 1-hour tours MWF, year-round; ages 7 and above recommended. Free. Self-guided also. ☀ *847-7333*

Summer (July/August) is peak season, and most popular, for this tour that includes a behind-the-scenes view of greenhouses and labs filled with experimental flowers. Off-season tour includes courtyard garden with fish pond. Limited restrooms; no gift shop; no sales to public. All those flowers can be spectacularly colorful, so don't forget your camera.

☀ NASA/Ames Research Center

Mountain View. Hwy 101, take the Moffett Field Rd. exit. Move to far left and follow road to 4-way stop. Left on Parsons Av.; follow signs to Visitor Center. 2-hour tours are given, twice weekly, at 9:30 a.m. and 1:30 p.m. For ages nine and older. Reservations necessary. Free. ☀ *(415) 604-6497*

You'll know you're close when you see the monstrous flight hangar from the freeway. During the tour you'll go inside one, as well as a flight simulator, a centrifuge and assorted research aircraft. You'll also see the world's largest wind tunnel. It's a two-hour, two-mile walk, so if you have small children, plan the time of your visit accordingly and don't forget the fold-up stroller.

☀ National Weather Service

21 Grace Hopper Av., Monterey. Hwy 1 North, Casa Verde exit to stop. Turn left to end of road (Fairgrounds Av.); go left at fairgrounds to Airport Rd. Rt. on Airport, 3/4 mile to Navy Annex. Bear rt; follow road to end; you'll see the weather service office on your left. Recommended for 6th grade & up. 6am-6pm, M-F. Free. ☀ *656-1710*

See how National Weather Service forecasters use Doppler radar to create forecasts. Learn about volunteer spotters and the role they play in reporting weather. This casual tour lasts as long as you have questions.

☀ Nob Hill Markets

Nob Hill has 25 locations in Northern California. Any store can be toured, with advance reservations. Tours last one hour and are intended for 2-30 people. Free. ☀ *842-6441*

Elementary-school children really enjoy seeing how a large, modern supermarket works. Watch a cake decorator at work, see how meats are cut, and sample goodies from each department you tour. Discover where the market's food comes from, and how it gets there.

✳ NUMMI (New United Motor Manufacturing, Inc.)

45500 Fremont Bd., Fremont. I-680, Auto Mall Pkwy exit west, then left on Fremont Bd. Park in visitors' lot, just off main gate (#5). Enter through front lobby. 1½-hour tour, for ages 10-up, given T-F, 9:30, 11:30 and first and last Mondays at 7pm. Shorts/ sandals prohibited; long pants/closed shoes recommended. Free. ✳ (510) 498-5764

How does a car become a car? Have your children make their best guess, then take the tour and see how their version of the process compares with the real thing.

✳ Salz Leathers

1040 River St., Santa Cruz, Hwy 101, Market St. Exit. Rt. on Water St., and rt. on River. One-hour tours for groups of 6 or more, by appointment. Not suitable for very small children. Comfortable shoes recommended. Open M-F, 10-5; Sat., 10-5. ✳ 423-1480

Salz Leathers is the oldest tannery in the West. This family-owned business has been producing premium quality leather since 1855, and provides leather to customers worldwide.

✳ San Jose Arena

525 W. Santa Clara St., San Jose. Guadalupe Pkwy, Hwy 87 south to W. Santa Clara Exit. Parking is available in ground-level and above-ground lots as well as in nearby lots. ✳ 999-5824

Standard tour is conducted Fridays only at 11 a.m; Adults, $4; Seniors/Students 12-18, $3; Children 5-11, $1.50; under 5 free. Special "SJ Sharkie" tours (led by "Sharkie," the Sharks' mascot) are conducted on weekends at 10 and 11:30. Adults, $5; Seniors/Students/Children, $4; under 5, free. Tours go behind the scenes to executive suites and stars' room, and more. Special tours that include tickets/dinner and private tour can also be arranged for minimum of 12; $55-$110/person.

✳ San Jose Mercury News

750 Ridder Park Dr., San Jose. 1½-hour tours begin at 10:30, weekdays. Appropriate for 3rd grade and up. Reservations. Unless your group is part of the Newspapers in Education (NIE) program, a $20 donation is requested. (The fee goes to support the NIE program in a local school.) ✳ 920-5000

Kids who enjoy learning how the world works will find this tour "really neat" (our small expert's assessment). Tours include a bit of history of the Mercury News, and then the neat stuff: the equipment used to publish the newspaper, some of the mechanics of publishing and editing, and the production area. Informative guides explain all and answer kids' questions with enthusiasm.

✳ Santa Clara Valley Water District — offers two tours:

Water Discovery Trail, *Vasona Lake Park, 298 Garden Hill Dr., Los Gatos* ✳ *265-2607*

Self-guided, 45-minute tour suitable for all ages begins at the marina at Vasona Reservoir and follows the southern end of the reservoir. Twelve full-color panels describe water cycle, conservation, treatment. Panels positioned for easy viewing. Free.

Rinconada Water Treatment Plant, *400 More Av., Los Gatos* ✳ *395-8121*

Led by chemists and treatment plant operators, this one-hour tour is for ages 8 and over. See a fresh water treatment plant in action. Free.

✳ US Geological Survey (Western Region)

345 Middlefield Rd., Menlo Park. From Hwy 101 take Willow Rd west (right) to Middlefield Rd. north to USGS. Weekdays, except national holidays, 9-4. One-hour, self-guided tours. Visitors are asked to enter designated buildings only. Park in any lot and start at any point. For elementary ages and older. Handicapped accessible, bicycle racks available, restrooms. Free. ✳ *(415) 853-8300*

If the kids enjoy rocks and maps, you've come to the right place. Exhibits include unusual rock collections, surveying and mapping instruments, a spectrum of maps, and an active work station for recording earthquake activity. This is a great place to pick up information for school projects, or to do research.

✳ Whole Foods Markets

1690 S. Bascom Av. Campbell. I-880, Hamilton Av. exit to the corner of Bascom/Hamilton. Open daily 8:30 to 9:30pm. Free. ✳ *371-5000*

Tours visit various departments; watch the trucking operation and get a feel for the daily workings of this six-location market. Two weeks' notice; 20-participant minimum.

This next place doesn't offer guided tours, but it's worth a stop, especially if your youngster enjoys woodworking, building (like Lincoln Logs, but the real thing) or neat, old tools:

✳ Southern Lumber

1402 S. 1st St., San Jose. I-280, 7th St. exit south; right on Alma to corner of 1st & Alma. Open M-F, 8-6; Sat, 8-5; Sun, 9-5.
✳ *294-2368*

Southern Lumber is a retail lumber yard, unusual for its large variety (45-50) species of hardwoods. Stop on the mezzanine to see a display of antique woodworking tools.

 # TRANSPORTATION

The first adventure in most small lives begins with "Let's go bye-bye!" Whether it's a first trip to Grandma's or an outing to the grocery store, getting there is half the fun for kids. Or rather, sometimes it <u>is</u> the fun! Anything that goes "vroom-vroom," rolls, soars, clip-clops or otherwise gets from here to there can be immensely exciting, and here are some adventures in and around the San Jose/Santa Clara Valley area to tantalize your young travellers.

✳ NASA/Ames Research Center

(see Tours of the Working World, above)

✳ Antique Fly-In Air Show

Watsonville Municipal Airport ✳ *496-9559*

Thrill to the sight of over 500 antique airplanes, plus air shows. Displays of rare and unique aircrafts takes place each year on Memorial Day Weekend.

✳ Palo Alto Airport

925 Embarcadero Rd., Palo Alto ✳ *(415) 856-7833*

See parked, taxiing and flying airplanes. Reservations required. 9-2, T-Th.

✳ California Antique Aircraft Museum

12777 Murphy Av. San Martin. Take Hwy 101 to San Martin Exit. Take an immediate left for one mile to museum. Open Sat., 10-2. Free. ✳ *683-2290*

Has your son always dreamed of being in a dogfight? Does your daughter dream about Amelia Earhardt? Don't miss this exhibit of antique aircraft, guaranteed to stir the soul of anyone who longs to take flight — but not in a 747.

✺ California International Airshow

Salinas Municipal Airport, 40 Mortensen, Salinas ✻ (408) 754-1983

Kids don't have to be aircraft enthusiasts to be thrilled by the Air Force Thunderbirds, Navy Blue Angels, Canadian Snowbirds, Soviet Migs, professional skydivers and aerobatics that have been part of the show in the past. Also featured are civilian and military crafts, hot air balloons, over 100 military and civilian static displays. All revenues benefit local charities.

✺ Uesugi Farms Pumpkin Patch & Strawberry Stand

14485 Monterey Rd., Morgan Hill ✻ 779-2078

The train ride can be the highlight of your visit to the farm in October, when the Pumpkin Patch opens. Besides the food products and family fun, there are also arts and crafts for exhibit and sale.

✸ Trains

All Aboard! Yes, riding the rails through unusual and sometimes breath-taking terrain ranging from mountains to beaches is still an option in California. Train rides are fun for the entire family. They'll bring back fond memories for the older set who have traveled via train, and perhaps kindle an interest in little adventurers who have not.

✺ Billy Jones Wildcat Railroad, Inc. (see Ch. 3, Parks)

Oak Meadow Park, off Hwy. 17 (880), on Blossom Hill Rd., Los Gatos ✻ 356-2729

Park open 8-Sunset; $3 vehicle fee. Call for price/schedule for train rides.

✺ Casa De Fruta (see Off the Beaten Path, above)

6680 Pacheco Pass Hwy., Hollister ✻ 637-779-2078

Narrow gauge train traverses this day-trip complex; $2.50/passenger for the 20-minute ride.

✺ Niles Canyon Railway

Corner Main St. & Kilkare Rd., Sunol. To reach boarding area, take Hwy 84 west from I-680 or east from I-880 to the township of Sunol. Get tickets at boarding area. ✻ (510) 862-9063

The Niles Canyon was known as the "transcontinental gateway into the Bay Area," during the days when the original transcontinental railroad made its final approach to the Bay Area through its valley. The line became part of the Southern Pacific Railroad as it remained for over 100 years until the route was abandoned. Today, thanks to the efforts of the Pacific Locomotive Association who purchased the land and restored a portion of the line, trains run again on the first and third Sundays of each month from 10-4. Niles Depot, 36997 Mission Bd., Fremont, is open on the first weekend of the month from 10-4. The 1904 depot, also restored by the PLA, includes a Railroad and Local History museum with a large model railroad layout.

(SAN JOSE CONVENTION AND VISITORS BUREAU)

Enjoy a ride through the giant redwoods on the Roaring Camp & Big Trees Railroad.

✳ Roaring Camp & Big Trees Narrow Gauge Railroad

Graham Hill and Mt. Hermon Rds., Felton. Open on varying schedule year-round. Adults, $12.50-$14.00, depending on route; ages 3-12, $9-$10.50, under 3 (on lap), free. Parking $4. ✳ *335-4484 or 335-4400*

Roaring Camp is a re-creation of an 1880s logging town, complete with covered bridge, nostalgic general store and old-fashioned lithograph shop. Historic steam trains from the 1900s chug through redwood forest to the top of Bear Mountain or past panoramic views of the San Lorenzo River and through mountain tunnels down to the Santa Cruz Beach Boardwalk.

✳ South Bay Historical Railroad Society

*1005 Railroad Av., Santa Clara. T, 6-9pm; Sat, 10-3. Donations, or
loans of railroad artifacts welcomed.* ✳ *243-3969*

The South Bay Historical Railroad Society (SBHRS) was founded in
1985 to preserve the heritage of American railroading. Between 1985-
92, the SBHRS renovated the historic Santa Clara Depot, its current
home. The depot's ticket office dates from 1863. There's a small railroad museum with artifacts and displays depicting local railroad usages
and practices, and displays of HO and N scale museum grade model
railroad layouts.

 # PETS, ANIMALS AND WILDLIFE

Are puppies made for little boys and girls, or is it the other way
around? And kittens, and fish and guinea pigs.... Animals attract children, there is no doubt about it; anyone who's ever tried to walk right
past a pet shop with children in tow can attest to that!

San Jose is a wonderful place for viewing animals — we've got the
ocean to the west, the spacious wildlife refuge surrounding the bay,
several working farms within our county and since we're on the Pacific
Flyway, bird viewing is always an adventure.

For a more expensive but unforgettable glimpse at wild animals,
Marine World/Africa USA is a day trip that your little naturalists will
talk about for a long time. Within a reasonable amount of time you can
also reach the **San Francisco** or **Oakland Zoos**, where you can view a
variety of exotic animals, birds and reptiles. If you want to stay closer to
home there is our own Kelley Park, which contains **Happy Hollow Park
and Zoo** (see Chapter 3, Parks).

If **feeding the ducks** is a favorite family activity, you can indulge at
many of the parks and playgrounds scattered throughout the area. At
Vasona Lake in Los Gatos you'll find ducks, geese and waterfowl. Nothing quite matches the excitement of a toddler's face as these semi-tame
creatures just about his own size nibble noisily out of his hand!

If your taste in animals runs more to the domestic, there are some
pet stores in the area that are a treat for youngsters. If you look under
Pet Supplies & Pets Retail in the Yellow Pages, you'll find several pages
of listings.

One local favorite is **Andy's Pet Shop**, 1280 The Alameda, San Jose,
(298-0840), a commercial pet store known for their selection of puppies
(local breeders only), kittens, birds, reptiles and a miniature tide pool.

For a great selection of birds you can enjoy a hands-on experience

There's something about abundance of wildlife right in our own backyard that can fool us into thinking these critters are here for our amusement. Be careful: wild animals, no matter how cute or appealing, are <u>wild</u>. Cute little squirrels or foxes ·can carry rabies. Be sure your children know the rules: don't approach wild animals. Don't try to touch a nice, tame-looking cow or horse either, even the ones in the neighbor's pasture; they spend their lives outdoors here, and can be as wild as any "wild" animal. If approached with clear ground-rules and a little common sense, your nature-viewing in the San Jose area will be an exciting, rewarding experience that your children will never forget.

at **Parrot Troopers**, 10869 North Wolf Road, Cupertino, (252-5078). They carry a variety of exotic birds, including cockatoos and macaws. They let you handle these beautiful creatures, but you have to wash you hands first at the little hand-washing station as you enter the store.

If you're a fish lover, you can visit **Bangkok Aquarium**, 1224 South Bascom Avenue, San Jose (293-4414), a tropical fish and hobby store with an assortment of display aquariums. They'll even arrange a tour for you if you call ahead, and they consult at no extra charge.

The Humane Society of Santa Clara County, 2530 Lafayette Street, Santa Clara (727-3383) is an ideal place to pick up a new pet, or just to visit. There are lots of dogs, cats and some unusual wildlife. Ask about their animal education classes.

❋ Animal Odds 'n' Ends...
...in alphabetical order

❋ Alum Rock Park (Youth Science Institute)
16240 Alum Rock Avenue, San Jose ❋ 258-4322

The institute, located within Alum Rock Park, offers a unique experience for kids and their families: Saturday Family Science Classes, a nature center, a live animal room with a variety of animals found at the Park, a rehab center for injured animals and collection of preserved birds. They also offer summer science camps.

✵ Coyote Point Museum

Coyote Point, San Mateo. T-Sat, 10-5; Sun, 12-5; Admission is $3 adults, $2 seniors, $1 students 6-17, under 6, free. There is also a $4 charge to enter Coyote Point Park. ✵ *(415) 342-7755*

They emphasize Bay Area ecology with interactive, hands-on displays. Their Wildlife Habitat is an exhibit of live animals, birds, snakes and amphibians.

✵ Emma Prusch Farm

647 South King Road, San Jose ✵ *926-5555*

This working farm raises a large variety of farm animals you can visit, as well as steer, pigs and sheep raised by the 4-H and FFA students (see Chapter 1, Attractions, for more information).

✵ Hayward Shoreline Interpretive Center

4901 Breakwater Avenue, Hayward ✵ *(510) 881-6751*

This small wildlife museum, located adjacent to 1,800 acres of bayland, offers interpretive information. For an adventure, you can hike the eight miles of trails (flat enough for small hikers), or perhaps mountain bike them, and observe the wildlife from the observation platform. Call ahead for a schedule of nature programs.

✵ Hidden Villa

26870 Moody Road, Los Altos Hills ✵ *(415) 949-8660*

Come see the farm animals on this 1,600-acre farm/preserve, and find out about their summer camp, where youngsters can care for the farm animals while learning all about them.

✵ Long Marine Lab and Aquarium

100 Shaffer Road, Santa Cruz. Open T-Sun, 1-4. Near Natural Bridges State Park, west end of Delaware Avenue. ✵ *429-4308*

Long Marine Lab is a research and instructional facility of the Santa Cruz campus of the University of California. There are docents available to lead you on a tour and answer questions you might have. Group tours (10 or more) are by reservation only. Exhibits describe the marine life and environment in Monterey Bay. The kids will be impressed with the Blue whale skeleton, and will enjoy browsing through the book and gift shop.

✳ Lucy Evans Bayland Interpretive Center
2775 Embarcadero Road, Palo Alto ✳ *321-2111*

Explore and learn about the wildlife of the Baylands, and discover the many small and large creatures which inhabit the area. Programs on the hour, Saturday and Sunday, with workshops and videos. On the boardwalk that extends from the Center over the marshy Baylands, you can experience the unique natural setting of the wetlands environment, and maybe see some of the creatures you've just learned about.

✳ McClellan Ranch Park
(see Ch. 3, Parks, Regional & County)

✳ Monarch Butterfly Migration – Natural Bridges State Park
2531 West Cliff Drive, Santa Cruz ✳ *423-4609*

Each year, thousands of Monarch butterflies migrate to and from this location. No one seems to know how long this has been going on or why they choose this particular area, but it's a sight to remember a lifetime. Beginning around October they will appear and stay until approximately February. There are special events celebrating both their arrival and departure (see Chapter 6, Festivals); tours are available.

✳ Nike Animal Rescue Foundation (NARF)
✳ *224-6273*

They don't have an official address where they can be found, but you can call and ask where they might show up next. NARF is a unique organization that takes in unwanted or lost animals, ensures that they are spayed or neutered, and then sells them via local pet stores. While waiting to be "adopted" these animals are cared for in foster homes. To purchase, foster or volunteer to work at a pet store, you can contact them at the above number. They encourage the participation of kids.

✳ Palo Alto Junior Museum and Zoo
1451 Middlefield Road, Palo Alto. 11:15am to 3pm, Sunday, 2:3 Open T-Sat, 10-5. Free. ✳ *(415) 329-2111*

Parents and kids alike will have fun at the Museum's art, clay and science classes (offered quarterly), or learning about animals at their live demonstrations. They offer many unique programs, such as the Native North-American Indian workshop and the paper-airplane contest.

✳ San Francisco Bay National Wildlife Refuge

Near Dumbarton Bridge and Highway 84 ✳ _(415) 792-3178_

Water plays such an important part in the development of the whole Bay Area, and at this vast refuge on the Bay, kids can learn about the wild creatures that inhabit this waterside environment, and their interdependency on it and on us. There's a lot to see and learn here. Begin at the Visitors' Center near Dumbarton Bridge, where you can get maps and information. Then head outdoors to observe a large variety of wildlife, including waterfowl, ducks and shorebirds; since the Refuge is on a major flyway, the inhabitants here change seasonally. The refuge is also home to two endangered species, the California Clapper (a species of water-fowl) and the Salt Marsh Harvest Mouse. Life in California is so comfortable, we tend to think that humans have a monopoly on land around the Bay; the Refuge is a place where kids can put attitudes like that in perspective.

✳ Villa Montalvo

15400 Montalvo Road, Saratoga ✳ _741-3421_

Best known as a Center For The Arts, a little known secret is that Villa Montalvo is also a bird sanctuary. Birds of many varieties can be found here year-round (see Chapter 2 for more information).

✳ Whale watching

The coast between Santa Cruz and Half Moon Bay offers ample opportunity to view gray whales when they are migrating (Fall-north to south; March-May, south to north). Some of the best watching is at Davenport on Greyhound Rock, just north of Santa Cruz; (408) 462-8333. There is a steep trail and staircase which lead to this spot. Quite a bit more expensive, but a great adventure, are the boat charters which can be taken out of Santa Cruz. For a fee you can observe the whales from alongside in a chartered boat. Contact the Santa Cruz chamber of Commerce for a listing of Charter Companies (423-1111).

SMALL ART MUSEUMS, GALLERIES AND ART CENTERS

San Jose is quickly taking its place in the nation as a significant center for the visual arts. Besides the "biggies," like the San Jose Museum of Art (see Chapter 1), there are many places around the San Jose area where you and your family can enjoy the excitement of original artwork by outstanding artists.

Art galleries offer families an opportunity to experience art in all its shapes and forms, modern as well as traditional, in a small, non-threatening setting. Less imposing or overwhelming than a museum, a gallery is a quiet place to make personal decisions about taste, and just have a good time. And unlike a museum, galleries are free. You can combine a gallery stop with another activity from this book, or for an illuminating trip through the world of art, hope from gallery to gallery; the comparisons between the different approaches to art can confuse, astound, excite and often help define your tastes in the visual arts. Here's a list of some of the art galleries in the San Jose/Santa Clara Valley area (addresses are in San Jose unless otherwise indicated). Go — look — enjoy!

African American Art, 1275 Piedmont Rd., in the Piedmont Shopping Center (272-3885)

Allegra Gallery, 374 South First St. Contemporary painting, drawing and sculpture by South Bay artists, with an emphasis on San Jose talent. (265-7289)

Allied Arts Guild, 75 Arbor Rd., Menlo Park. The galleries in this collection of gardens, fountains, shops and Spanish-style buildings exhibit the early arts of handweaving, needlework, pottery and painting, and benefit the Packard Children's Hospital at Stanford. (415/325-3259)

Apogee Gallery, 14527 Ramstad Dr. (251-5897)

Art Emporium, 71 N. San Pedro (295-2565)

Artbeat Gallery, 122 El Paseo de Saratoga. (374-7008)

Artist's Eye, The, (946-0957)

Beverly's Fine Art, 95 W. Main Ave., Morgan Hill (779-1235)

Bingham Gallery, 170 S. Market St. (993-1066)

Brookings Gallery, 330 Commercial St. (287-3311)

Cahn Gallery, Los Gatos (356-0023)

California Art Gallery & Collectible Center, 3155 S. Bascom Av., Campbell (559-6722)

California Frame-ups, 10123 N. Wolfe Rd., Cupertino (255-5592)

Chabot Gallery, 2068 Valico Fashion Park, Cupertino (255-4272)

Citadel Gallery, 855 S. Fifth St. Works by local emerging artists. (244-1692)

Collectair Aviation Art Gallery, Reid Hillview Airport (259-3360)

Creative Valley Art Center, 3161 Humboldt Ave., Santa Clara (985-2655)

Deck the Walls, 2652 Town Center Ln., Sunnyvale (735-9699)

DeSilva Gallery, 71 N. San Pedro (998-1300)

Elsa's Studio and Gallery, 1880 Forest Ave. (287-6595)

Fong Galleries, 383 S. 1st St. (298-4141)

Gallery Morgan Hill, 17490 Monterey Rd., Morgan Hill (776-7990)

Gallery Saratoga, 112 El Paseo Shopping Center. A cooperative that features local artists. (866-0884)

Goose Pond Gallery, 17375 S. Monterey Rd., Morgan Hill (779-4306)

Granovsky Gallery, Fairmont Hotel, 170 S. Market St. Contemporary Russian, European and American art. (295-3388)

Lacoste Gallery, 227 N. First St. Contemporary European and Bay Area artists. (295-5706)

Macchu Picchu Folk Art and Gallery of the Americas, 42 S. 1st St. (280-1860)

Me Productions, 1140 Pedro St. Specialists in wall graphics. (947-1881)

Refuge, The, 205 Town and Country Village. Wildlife and western art. (244-2991)

San Jose Art Center, 482 S. 2nd St. (294-4545)

San Jose Art League's Downtown Gallery, 14 S. 1st St. (287-8435)

San Jose Institute of Contemporary Art, 450 S. Market St. (283-8155) and 2 N. 2nd St. (998-4310)

San Jose Museum of Art, 110 S. Market St. (294-2787) See Chapter 1.

San Jose State University Art Galleries, One Washington Square (north of San Carlos, near 9th Street). (924-4328)

Thomas Kinkade Gallery, Valley Fair Mall (244-5889)

Works Gallery, 260 Jackson St. (295-8378)

Young Gallery, 307 N. Santa Cruz Ave., Los Gatos (399-1900)

Z Gallery, 2855 Stevens Creek Bd., Santa Clara (984-2511)

Of course, you don't have to go specifically to a gallery to enjoy the creative arts. San Jose has a wonderful program of **Art in Public Places**, which means that you might happen upon some outstanding works when you least expect it, outside. Love it, hate it — everyone has a personal reaction to public art, and experiencing it first-hand can help develop and hone your youngsters' artistic tastes. Here's a partial list of some of the surprises; if this whets your family's appetite, call the Cultural Affairs office of the City of San Jose for up-to-the-moment information: (277-5144). (The numbers on this list correspond to the numbered locations on the map on the next page.)

1. Fairmont Plaza *Steel sculpture*
2. Federal Building *Bronze memorial*
3. State Office Building *Three sculptures in various media*
4. Technology Center of Silicon Valley "Garage" *Audio-kinetic sculpture*
5. Convention Center *Five sculptures in various media*
6. Center for the Performing Arts *Four sculptures in various media*
7. Children's Discovery Museum *Marble relief mural*
8. Plaza Park *Granite and glass fountain*
9. Guadalupe River Bridge/Park Avenue *Bronze sculpture*
10. McEnery Park *Sculpture of cement, wood and metal*
11. Mitsubishi Bank *Stainless steel sculpture*
12. Almaden Blvd. at Santa Clara St. *Stainless steel sculpture*
13. Pacific Western Building *Four sculptures*
14. Market-Post Tower *Bronze sculpture*
15. Sixty South Market *Three sculptures in various media*
16. 95 South Market *Painted metal sculpture*
17. Park Center Plaza *Five sculpture in various media*
18. Exhibit Hall *Two sculptures*
19. Fifth and Taylor Streets *Sculpture of steel, paint and concrete*

(See accompanying map next page for locations.)

 # SHOPPING AND HOBBIES

 ## Toys and other Kid Stuff

If you can play with it, climb on it, throw it, catch it, wear it, listen to it or otherwise have fun with it, you can probably find it in one of the many centers of these toy-store giants: Kay-Bee Toys (Oakridge, Eastridge, Westgate, Vallco and The Great Mall), Toys "R" Us (1082 Blossom Hill Road, Saratoga-Sunnyvale Road at El Camino Real; 330 North Capitol Avenue; and 751 South Winchester Boulevard).

If you prefer to browse in a small, less warehouse-like atmosphere,

Art in Public Places

1 Fairmont Plaza

2 Federal Building

3 State Office Building

4 Technology Center of Silicon Valley "Garage"

5 Convention Center

6 Center for the Performing Arts

7 Children's Discovery Museum

8 Plaza Park

9 Guadalupe River Bridge/Park Avenue

10 McEnery Park

11 Mitsubishi Bank

12 Almaden Blvd. at Santa Clara St.

13 Pacific Western Building

14 Market-Post Tower

15 Sixty South Market

16 95 South Market

17 Park Center Plaza

18 Exhibit Hall

19 Fifth and Taylor Streets

or if you're looking for something more personalized or more unusual, try some of the shops listed below. You won't find as vast an array as you would at "the giants," but you may be surprised at the creative, unusual toys and games you will find.

✳ Affordable Treasures

748 Blossom Hill Road, Los Gatos ✳ *356-3101*

This is the place to find party give-aways for your next birthday party, as well as a wide variety of party supplies, like pinatas, and carnival and novelty items.

✳ Bears In The Woods

59 North Santa Cruz, Los Gatos ✳ *354-6974*

In business for over 19 years, this teddy-bear store has every type of teddy-bear item imaginable. They also have a "Safari" room with gift items of endangered species. A portion of the proceeds from sales in the "Safari" room go toward an endangered species foundation.

And if teddy-bears are the absolute passion of someone in your house, you might want to consider a weekend trip to Nevada City in April for the annual Teddy Bear Convention. Bears come literally from all over the world for this delightful, whimsical weekend filled with bears in every shape, form and size, plus all the bear-aphernalia that goes with them. If you love a bear-lover, find out about this; (916) 265-5804.

✳ The Disney Store

2855 Stevens Creek Boulevard (In Valley Fair Center) ✳ *241-7377*

Everything is Disney here. When they're not playing a Disney video, they play Disney music. Clerks dress in costume and the store is filled with Disney items, past and present, including all kinds of toys and games which reflect everyone's favorite Disney characters.

✳ Imaginarium

182 Oakridge Mall, San Jose ✳ *629-7498 and 2855 Stevens Creek Boulevard (Valley Fair Shopping Center)* ✳ *249-1070*

This is a learning center and a toy store in one, that promotes active participation with the toys; your kids get to test everything before you buy it. You can find computer learning games, science games, puzzles, discovery kits, wooden toys, ant farms and just about anything else you can think of that involves the imagination.

✳ Kiddie World Toys

3640 Stevens Creek Boulevard ✳ *241-1100*

One of the largest (non-chain) toy stores in the area, they've got a great variety and it's not just all trendy toys, although they do carry the most popular ones. You'll also find some unique toys here.

✳ Kitty 'n' Friends

10123 North Wolfe Road, Cupertino (In Vallco Fashion Park) ✳ *255-4912*

What child doesn't love things in miniature? If your kids enjoy teeny-tiny toys, they'll love Kitty's tiny note pads, little pens & pencils and all kinds of (primarily pink) fun items. Most kids are drawn to this store as they pass and can spend lots of time browsing.

✳ Lin's Toy Cupboard

237A State Road, Los Altos ✳ *(415) 948-4511*

This store specializes in unusual versions of common toys, such as dolls and bears, many of which are collectibles for kids as well as adults. "Vanderbears," which are stuffed fuzzy bears with their own clothing, are one of the most popular items. "Gotz" and "Corolle" dolls are two other specialties. They carry a variety of other toys for children ages 0-13.

✳ Sesame Street General Store

2855 Stevens Creek Road, Santa Clara (in Valley Fair Shopping Center) ✳ *247-8676*

You'll find toys for learning here, everything from computerized learning toys to flash cards and books. There is also a wide assortment of kids' clothing and stuffed animals.

✳ Wiz Kids

647 East Calaveras Boulevard, Milpitas ✳ *934-1890*

For whiz kids between 4 and 18, you can find chemistry sets, software, telescopes, test sets, music and other hands-on, educational fun stuff.

✳ The Wooden Horse

798 Blossom Hill Road, Los Gatos ✳ *356-8821*

Their specialty is active, hands-on toys that promote the imagination and creative play. A few of the more novel items they carry are unusual wooden rocking horses and a line of toys called, "Creativity for Kids", a special line of crafts kits for kids.

✳ Factory Outlet Shopping

The Outlets at Gilroy

Hwy 101 and Leavesley Road

There are over 75 stores here including Carters, Esprit, Guess?, LA Gear and Oshkosh B'Gosh. And these are just a few that have loads of kids' things. There's much more to see and as of this printing there's a new section underway.

You'll also find several factory outlet stores at the Great Mall of the Bay Area (see below).

✳ Food and Supermarkets

Shopping for food is one of life's necessities — and can be an educational, cultural or just plain fun experience. Shopping is easy in the San Jose area. Many of the large supermarkets are "Superstores" where you can buy just about anything under the same roof — groceries, clothing, drugs, magazines, liquor, and fresh-baked goods. Taking care of life's necessities just doesn't get much easier!

Like anything else we do often, we can get in a rut when it comes to buying food. Avoid the food-shopping "blah's" by sampling different markets. Some have food samples, some decorate for whatever holiday is coming up, and some just have a different atmosphere.

Safeway is a popular supermarket chain that offers, fresh produce, exotic fruits and vegetables (by season), and everything else you'd expect to find in a super-store. **Lucky's** Supermarkets does the same, but claims to do it cheaper. And for "warehouse supermarket" shopping try **Pak N Save** and **Food 4 Less**; big savings, no frills, you bag your own (this can be an adventure for little shoppers).

If you're looking for something a little more out of the ordinary, try **Nob Hill**, **Petrini's**, **Cosentino's** or **Trader Joe's**. These markets offer more up-scale, exotic and sometimes foreign items... the more expensive.

Whole Earth Foods, previously known as **The Bread of Life**, is an alternative grocery store that specializes in all natural foods; no preservatives, steroids, chemicals etc. If your kids accompany you regularly to the ordinary supermarket, this can be an interesting change. They can practice weighing, scooping, bagging and other fun stuff. They even have mini-shopping carts so the kids can push their own.

✳ Hobbies

What was your hobby when you were a kid? Don't remember?... or you had so many you can't remember which was your favorite? Kids are inveterate collectors, and love to try new things — just put a kid in a kitchen with a basket full of pourable or measurable ingredients, and watch what happens!

You'll find lots of Hobby shops listed in the Yellow Pages under "Hobby & Model Construction Supplies – Retail." There are numerous hobby shops in the area. So, if your kids don't have a specific hobby you can shop around a bit and find one that best fits their interests. Here's a small sampling:

✳ **Castle Hobbies**, *1008 Blossom Hill Road* ✳ *265-3610*, specializes in radio-controlled (RC) cars, planes, and boats. They also sell models. Terry Scott, the store's owner, is very involved in sponsoring different groups that race on weekends. You can watch RC cars race at the CCOC (Vocational school) campus, Hwy 87 at Capitol the third Sunday of each month. They start at about 9am. There are also boat races (sailboats) at Helyer Park, Capitol Avenue at Helyer, about every other Saturday. The Tom Cats is the name of the organization that flies/races RC planes at Santa Clara County Model Aircraft Sky Park, 9800 Lantz Drive in Morgan Hill.

✳ **The Game Gallery**, *in Valley Fair Mall, Hwy 880 at Stevens Creek Boulevard, Santa Clara* ✳ *241-4263*, has over 3000 games to choose from. If games of any kind are your hobby, you should be able to find one here to suit you. They've got board games, computer games, jigsaw puzzles, darts, fantasy and war games....

If your child has always had a fascination with trains, there are two stores in the area that should delight them: **The Great Train Store**, (956-1797) in the Great Mall in Milpitas, and **The Train Shop**, (296-1050) at the corner of Winchester and Pruneridge in Santa Clara, both have models, books, videos, and other train-related collectibles.

If you're looking for something a little unusual, try **Helicopter World**

Inc. in Milpitas, (942-9521). They have over 40 radio-controlled helicopters on display, and are said to be the largest supplier of RC helicopters in the region. **Slammers and Pogs,** in The Great Mall, Milpitas (945-7647) is a trendy store specializing in the sale of new pogs and slammers. Your kids can tell you all about this craze if you're not already aware.

If you have a little collector who just happens to love cats, try **Purrsnickety** in Los Gatos (395-2287). You'll find everything you can imagine: ceramic cats, cat T-shirts, cat hats, cat purses, and of course stuffed kitties.

Michael's can always be a great source of ideas; here you'll find acres of arts and crafts materials. It's fun just to try to imagine what some of them are for! Michael's has five locations in the San Jose area.

Is sewing a hobby, or a necessity? Or both? Or just plain fun? See "Fabric Shops" in the Yellow Pages for the listing of over forty fabric stores in our area. Many of them have classes for beginners, craft kits, and special holiday projects.

❋ Hardware Stores

This is where the individual bits and pieces of our homes and gardens are displayed for us to piece back together — or simply examine with wonder. Grown-ups tend to take it all too seriously; kids find all sorts of treasures in these aisles, and a trip to the hardware store can re-charge their "mystery" batteries!

ACE Hardware is your neighborhood hardware store, chock-full of "neat stuff." You'll find several ACE locations in the telephone directory. Kids love to plunge their hands into the bins of "little things" — nails, bolts, shiny this or that, brass doo-hickeys — and always find something to touch, examine, listen to, or just plain wonder about. For a real insight into just how dull and predictable grown-ups tend to be, don't tell them what each item is for: instead, ask how many different things they think it could be used for. Their imaginative responses can be a real eye-opener!

Orchard Supply Hardware (OSH) has many locations throughout the area and sells household items as well as materials for do-it-yourself projects. They also have a garden section. **Home Depot** is the hardware giant. There have locations in Milpitas, San Jose and Santa Clara. The aisles are huge, the ceilings high and the kids will marvel at not only the selection but the fork lifts and machines required to move all of it around.

Soko Hardware and Plumbing Co. is a unique cultural experience in hardware. Located at 565 North 6th Street, downtown San Jose, this hardware store is like no other in the area. It is in the heart of JapanTown and so carries items specific to the Japanese culture. You'll find Japanese cooking utensils, building materials, beautiful crockery, pottery and much more. You might want to ask some questions.

💥 School and Office Supplies

Although children quickly get tired of using school supplies for homework, they never tire of looking at new ones! They can cruise the aisles of office supply stores for hours, finding all kinds of gizmos and gadgets that make "playing school" or "playing office" more fun. **McWhorter's Stationers** with 20 locations throughout the Bay area has by far the largest inventory of office supplies around. They have everything from paperclips and notebooks to furniture and gift ideas. **Teachers' Helper Inc.**, 5353 Prospect Road and **Teacher's Supply House Learning Rainbow Inc.** are just two of the school supply stores in the area. There is a veritable treasure-trove of stickers, papers, notebooks, workbooks, gradebooks, puzzles, and things that make learning fun. See the Yellow Pages under School Supplies for further listings.

💥 Sporting Goods

The San Jose area is a sportsman's paradise, and there are shops all over where you can get supplies for just about any sport you can name. At these establishments, you can learn about whatever activity intrigues your little sportsperson, examine equipment, try it on, buy or rent and find out where to use it.

One of the biggest is **R.E.I.** (Recreational Equipment Inc.) at 20640 Homestead Road, Cupertino (446-1991). They sell and rent equipment and clothing, and have up-to-date recreational information for the entire region. **Oshman's** has four locations, San Jose, Santa Clara and Mountain View and Milpitas. They have quality outdoor equipment as well as anything you could want for sporting activities. Their largest location in the Great Mall of Milpitas has a lot of hands-on-activities: you can try tennis, golf, archery, basketball or rock climbing at any of their in-store practice facilities. **Big 5 Sporting Goods** in Milpitas, Sunnyvale, and San Jose specializes is sports equipment and carries many hard-to-find items, from knee braces to binoculars and everything in between.

Some of the other sporting goods stores you won't want to miss are: **Mel Cottons**, 1266 W. San Carlos, San Jose (281-5994), which specializes in camping gear and supplies for sale or rent; **Tri-City**, 40900

Grimmer Boulevard in Fremont (510/851-9600), the largest sporting goods store in Fremont; **The Sports Fanatic**, 717 El Camino Real, Sunnyvale (733-7757), with equipment for just about every sport you can think of; and **Play It Again Sports** (three locations in the area), which specializes in the sale and purchase of used sports equipment.

✹ Malls

Shopping malls have become the "downtown" of today's world. With their restaurants, cinemas, walking courses, entertainment centers and other amenities, they attract people for shopping, strolling, dining, "going out" and just having fun together. You don't need to spend a fortune to spend the day at the mall. Here are some of the more popular sights for shoppers in and around the San Jose area.

✷ **Stanford Shopping Center**, *180 El Camino Real, Palo Alto* ✷ *(415) 617-8585.* Directly across from Stanford University, this beautiful outdoor shopping mall has over 140 specialty stores, and award-winning landscaping that creates a garden-like atmosphere. It's a very relaxing place to stroll and shop.

✷ **Valley Fair Shopping Center**, *2855 Stevens Creek Boulevard, Santa Clara* ✷ *248-4451.* With over 170 stores, including Macy's, Nordstrom and Emporium, it's easy to see why this is a favorite with the adults. It also stores for the kids, like the Disney Store, Warner Brothers and Sesame Street Stores. Their food court offers so much variety that everyone in the family can try something different with very little effort.

✷ **The Great Mall of the Bay Area**, *near Highways 680, 880 and 101 in Milpitas* ✷ *(956-2033),* was once Ford Motor Company's Auto Manufacturing Plant and is now said to be one of California's largest outlet malls. Tucked among the hundreds of specialty shops you'll find classic cars and travel displays. There is a 700-seat international food court, and with Wonderpark, a state-of-the-art family entertainment center, right in the mall, none of the kids should complain about going shopping. Its circular floor plan allows you to visit every store without backtracking.

✷ **Vallco Fashion Park**, *at Interstate 280 and Wolfe Road in Cupertino* ✷ *255-5660.* Kids love this place which has a complete family fun center, Tilt, and one of the areas nicest ice skating rinks, Ice Capades Chalet. Over 170 stores including, Sears, Emporium, JC Penney's and Ross.

✸ **Sunnyvale Town Center**, *on Mathilda and Washington Avenues in Sunnyvale* ✸ *245-6585*, has a unique courtyard where shoppers can sit among redwood trees to relax and rest their feet. 121 shops and a theater complex.

✸ **Oakridge Mall**, *Highway 85 and Santa Teresa Boulevard, San Jose* ✸ *578-2910.* Not nearly as crowded as most, Oakridge has over 110 stores including Macy's, Montgomery Wards and Nordstrom, a Cinema with bargain mid-week rates and a variety of places to eat.

✸ **Eastridge Shopping Center** *at the corner of Tully Road and Capitol Expressway* ✸ *238-3600.* Located on the east side of San Jose, this mall includes Macy's, JC Penney's, Emporium, Sears and 160 other speciality stores. Highlights for kids include the grand-court glass elevator, a community room, an antique carousel, a water fountain with and hourly water show, the Food Pavilion and an enclosed ice skating area next to Emporium.

✸ Odds and Ends

If you haven't found what you're looking for at one of San Jose's many malls, or if you prefer a smaller-scale, more personalized shopping experience, try some of these places for something different. (For collectible or second hand items, try any of the outdoor flea markets and auctions in the Outdoor Markets section of this chapter.)

Baby Super Rocker World
1523 Parkmoore Avenue ✸ *293-0358*

One of the area's largest baby and children's stores, they also have the area's widest selection of rocking chairs. Making up your mind can be a very pleasurable experience as you try them all out.

Buttons and Bows
6055-J Meridian Avenue ✸ *927-6614*

A great place to find what they call "gently used" kids' clothes. They buy and sell a large assortment of clothing for all ages. They also have a kids' play area to keep the troops occupied while you shop. They obviously know kids!

Kimono My House
1424 62nd Street, Emeryville ✸ *(510) 428-0922*

The world's biggest selection of Japanese Science Fiction and robot toys. They call it Japanimation. You'll find models, t-shirts posters, and of course the ever-popular Godzilla.

Media Play

940 Great Mall Drive, Milpitas ✻ *934-1844*

This store is an adventure that media-oriented kids will appreciate. Located in the Great Mall in Milpitas, Media Play gives kids a chance to try out video games, CD's and books before they buy them. There are benches and chairs set up where you can relax and browse through books, video monitors where you can play the games, and headphones for sampling the latest CD's. They also have a coffee bar where Mom or Dad can help relax while the kids enjoy.

The Playground Outlet

850 East El Camino Real, Sunnyvale ✻ *737-7497*

Play equipment is the name of the game here. They specialize in all kinds of playground equipment, as the name implies, and make most of theirs out of California redwood and southern yellow pine (very sturdy woods).

Yaohan USA

675 Saratoga Av. ✻ *255-6690*

One of the biggest grocery/super-stores in Japan has a branch in San Jose. You can find food, housewares, pottery, clothing, shoes, toys, CDs and tapes, books, and even a place to have an authentic Japanese meal (fast-food style). If you've never been to Japan, this is a real cultural treat! If you have, this will bring it all back.

✸ Thrift/Consignment Stores

Thrift stores can be an adventure for young or old. Treasures can lurk among the humdrum, and "previously owned" can mean simply that someone else loved it before you had a chance to. Prices can be unbeatable, too! Some consignment stores carry new items as well.

Two consignment stores that offer a wide selection of children's clothing are **Once Around Resale Shop**, 18480 Prospect Road, Saratoga (252-6068) and **Once Upon A Child**, 1929 El Camino Real, Mt. View, (415) 960-6822. They also have varying assortments of used play equipment, furniture, cribs, strollers, games and decorations.

The proceeds from thrift stores often go toward worthy causes, so if you enjoy helping people as well as shopping, you might want to stop in at the following stores. **Happy Dragon Thrift Shop**, 245 West Main Street, Los Gatos (354-4072), has great goodies to sift/shop through, and donates all proceeds to the Eastfield Ming Quong (a residential mental-health facility for ages 8-18). **The Youth Science Institute Thrift Store**, 3151 Alum Rock Avenue (272-1301), is sponsored by the Alum Rock Park Youth Science Institute and all proceeds go toward this worthwhile center (see chapter 3, Parks).

 # CHILD PHOTOGRAPHERS

There are moments in every child's life that we cherish and want to save for posterity. Many photographers in the San Jose/Santa Clara Valley area specialize in children, or are simply known for always doings a good job getting their fidgety subjects to cooperate. Here's a partial list; check the Yellow Pages under Photographers for more. And don't forget "the giants," like K-Mart, Sears, J.C. Penney and Montgomery Ward. Their children's specials can make it worth the wait, and their photographers are often quite experienced at getting kids to stop moving and smile.

Deborah Stern Photography, 20 S. Santa Cruz Ave., Los Gatos
395-1620

Expressly Portraits, 1 (800) 34-1-HOUR. Many locations; call for the one nearest you.

Lisa Fenwick Photography, 659 15th Ave., Menlo Park
(415) 326-8659

Genesis Photography, 185 Moffett Bd., Mountain View
(415) 967-2301

Ken Green Photography, 260 S. Sunnyvale Ave., Ste. 8, Sunnyvale
720-9577

Kids Klub Portrait Studios, 2283 Lincoln Ave., San Jose 978-7300

Kinderfoto Portrait Studio, Oakridge Mall, 224-8454; Sunnyvale Town Center, 749-1648

Mary Kroeger Photography, 285 Sobrante Way, Suite G, Sunnyvale
749-1400

Olan Mills Portrait Studios, 4750 Almaden Expwy 265-0860; Food for Less Shopping Center 223-2773; 1814 Hillsdale Av. 723-0477; Westgate West Shopping Center 996-1931; Kiely Plaza, Santa Clara 984-2432

Arthur F. Mintz Photography, 20490 Saratoga-Los Gatos Rd., Saratoga
867-4077

Sheldon Photographers, 380 Main St., Los Altos (415) 948-3823; (800) 948-3823

 # HOTEL HOPPING

Traveling can be exciting, even if it's someone else doing it. Big hotels are filled with people from all over, people rushing about, enjoying life, working hard and simply on the move. New ideas can grow from new faces; a change of scenery is sometimes exactly what's called for. So whether your little tourists are suffering from cabin fever, rainy weather blues or just need a change of pace, you'll find distractions, good food and who knows what exciting things to see by visiting some of San Jose's fine hotels.

If you're in the downtown area, you can do a lot of hopping. Start with **The Fairmont Hotel,** 170 South Market Street (998-1900), located across from Cesar Chavez Park. The clientele here is a mix of business and pleasure; many conference-goers to the near-by Convention Center stay here. You can sit in the sunken area in the center of the hotel and enjoy nightly bands. The restaurant has a children's menu, with items ranging from $6-10. For guests, they have baby-sitting upon request, and free crayons and coloring books at the front desk.

Downtown's newest hotel is the **Hilton,** 300 Almaden Boulevard (287-2100). They have a complete children's menu ranging from $6-8, about half the price of their adult menu items. Like most Hiltons, this one offers prime people-watching, neat elevators, and occasionally, live music. And like most big hotels, their holiday decorations can be worth a stop; during the holiday season you might check to see if there are any special performances or celebrations.

Just down the street, in the center of the downtown area, is the Historic **DeAnza Hotel,** 233 West Santa Clara Street (286-1000). Built in 1930's, this hotel is now a local landmark. The restored interior of the lobby is beautiful, and the staff will be more than happy to show you around if you ask.

The **Hyatt St. Clair,** 302 South Market Street, San Jose (295-2000), also a downtown landmark, is the oldest restored hotel in town (restorations were done by the same man who did the original work in the early 1920's). Their restaurant, Il Fornaio, has a children's menu with items starting at $5.00.

MOVIE TRIVIA

Many well-known Hollywood flicks have been filmed in and around San Jose. See how many of these settings you recognize during your travels.

✳ St. Thomas Aquinas Church, 745 Waverley St. Palo Alto's oldest church (1902), a Gothic Revival building, was used as a location in "Harold & Maude."

✳ Prior to World War I, Niles (Ch. 7, Day Trips-Fremont) was the home of Essanay Studios, owned by Bronco Billy. Bronco Billy's studio produced westerns as well as the notable Chaplin film, "Little Tramp," in which Charlie Chaplin perfected his "Chaplin walk." Other stars of Essanay Studios included Wallace Beery, Chester Conklin and Ben Turpin. Many cowboy adventures were filmed in the Niles Canyon and on the main streets of Niles. Charlie Chaplin Day is celebrated on the first Saturday in June. Family activities include silent movies, look-alike contest prizes, sidewalk sale, cake walks and more.

✳ Arnold Schwarzenegger needed to blow up an unfinished building for his movie, "Terminator II," and Fremont (Ch. 7, Day Trips-Fremont) had just what he wanted.

✳ Mission San Juan Bautista was the setting for Alfred Hitchcock's "Vertigo," released in 1958. (Ch. 7, Day Trips, and Ch. 8, Missions).

✳ Tim Conway is known for his serialized "Julius Dorff" movies. "Julius Dorff's First Olympics" was shot at San Jose's Egyptian Museum (Ch. 1).

✳ Remember Robin Williams' great court scene in "Mrs. Doubtfire"? It was shot at the Redwood City County Courthouse.

✳ Several episodes of the "Star Man" series were shot at the Lick Observatory (Ch. 2, Planetariums) on Mt. Hamilton, San Jose. Star Man takes his son to the observatory to show him where he came from.

✳ "The Candidate," starring Robert Redford, was filmed in part at San Jose's Eastridge Mall. Maybe you'll spot something familiar during a shopping foray (Ch. 2, Shopping).

✳ "The Wash," an independent feature and "American Playhouse Special," was filmed in San Jose's Japantown, an area between 4th and 6th Sts., and Taylor and Empire Sts. (Ch. 2).

✳ "Beverly Hills Cop III" and "Getting Even With Dad," starring Macaully Culkin, were filmed at Great America (see Ch. 1). You'll probably recognize this location.

✳ "Getting Even With Dad" also filmed some scenes at Raging Waters (Ch. 1).

 # ON THE HORIZON

Just when you think you've seen and done it all here, something new and exciting pops up! By the time this book reaches your hands, the San Jose area will most likely be just a little different than it is now. Some of the entries below may already be realities. Some of these ideas may have disappeared entirely, to be replaced by other, new and exciting possibilities. One thing to remember: When looking for things to do in the Santa Clara Valley, always keep an eye on the horizon.

✳ Bay Area Ridge Trail

The Bay Area Ridge Trail Council is currently creating a multiple-use trail along the ridgetops surrounding the San Francisco Bay. As of this printing, 190 miles of the natural, recreational trail are open. Explore wonderful views, rugged ridges, rolling hills, alpine lakes...all from the planned 400-mile ridgeline trail right in our backyard. Call or write the Council for a quarterly listing of organized hikes, mountain bike rides and horseback rides: 311 California St., Suite 300, San Francisco, CA 94104; (415) 391-0697.

✳ Other trails

See Chapter 3, Parks, Playgrounds and other Outdoor Fun, for a listing of trails that are currently being developed. They'll range in difficulty from easy to strenuous, and offer endless possibilities for burning off that energy that seems to wane only when it comes to picking up socks.

✳ Garlic Country USA

Not everyone agrees that this proposed park at the junction of Highways 101 and 152 is right for the area. Dining, shopping and lots of entertainment are on the slate for this mammoth entertainment center near Gilroy, which will be about twice the size of Disneyland and will offer restaurants, shops and twelve music theaters. Imagine the Gilroy Garlic Festival, every day of the year!

✸ Guadalupe River Park

Watch for exciting developments in this riverside park. Until now it's been largely undeveloped, and is used as the site of concerts and outdoor events. Keep an eye on the media for the direction these plans are going to take.

✸ Shakespeare in the Park

The city of Cupertino will begin offering free performances of Shakespeare's plays in Memorial Park beginning the summer of 1996. Watch your local newspapers for developments and schedules, or call 777-3217 (Cupertino City) or (415) 666-2222 (San Francisco Shakespeare Theater).

3
Parks, Playgrounds and Other Outdoor Fun

San Jose is an outdoor kind of place. But even we were surprised to find that there are over 125 parks throughout the San Jose area. That speaks well for the quality of life here, and for our priorities. A trip to the playground is the biggest adventure for small children; and everyone in the family can enjoy an outing at the park or an adventure along a trail, a picnic, some badminton or catch, roller skating or simply relaxing in the shade of an old tree... San Jose has lots to choose from. The following list is far from complete; but these will get you started. And although playgrounds are most often found in parks, the two are not always synonymous, so they are listed separately to facilitate your search. First...

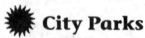 City Parks

Of the more than 125 parks in our area, several of them are City Parks which have a variety of features and activities to offer, ranging from a wildlife center and a cultural garden to a zoo and a historical museum. Any of these beautiful parks make for a delightful, all-day family adventure, and the price is definitely right. You can even reserve a picnic site by calling (408) 277-4191. Maps and additional information: (408) 27-PARKS.

Almaden Lake Park

Almaden Expressway and Coleman Avenue. 8 am to sunset. Fees: $3 parking, two-man paddle boat $8 an hour, three man $10. ✹ *277-5130*

There's something for everyone here: picnic areas, barbecues, playgrounds, paddle boats, biking trails, horseshoes, and the only sand beach and swimming in the area. Picnic areas are available on a first come, first serve basis. Walk, run or ride bikes along the nearby Los Alamitos Creek Trail. A small concession stand sells snacks and cold drinks.

Alum Rock Park

16240 Alum Rock Avenue. 8am to one-half hour after sunset. Take Highway 680 to the Alum Rock exit East; the road dead ends at the park. Fees: $3.00 parking, horse rentals $17.50 for an hour and $25 for one and one-half hours. ✹ *277-5477*

Alum Rock Park, founded in 1872, is the oldest regional park in the area. In the late 1800s it was best known as a health spa, with 27 mineral springs, an indoor swimming pool, restaurant and dance pavilion; but it quickly became overused and impossible to maintain.

Today the park is known for its lush vegetation, hiking trails, wildlife, and other features scattered throughout its 720 acres of hills, canyons and creek bed. Your family can enjoy hiking, horseback riding, bicycling, picnicking and a playground for younger children.

Come ready to exercise: there are more than 13 miles of hiking trails. Be sure to keep an eye on your small children, since some areas can be steep and there is some poison oak off the main trails. Trails are very well marked for your safety. The kids will love the Creek Trail, which runs along what was once the old electric railroad that brought the well-to-do to the famous spa. Remnants of the old mineral spas are also a popular site.

Other special features include clean picnic areas with barbecue facilities; a Visitors Center, complete with first aid station and nature displays; the Youth Science Institute; and a unique outdoor rope-course used by groups to build a sense of teamwork.

Emma Prusch Farm Park

647 South King Road, East San Jose. 8:30 am to sunset. Free.
✱ *277-5435*

At 47 acres, this is the largest farm in San Jose. Farm animals (chickens, pigs, sheep, rabbits, deer and ducks), 100 community garden plots, a display of old farm equipment, a rare fruit orchard, and lots of open space to run, fly kites or have a picnic. Special events include: gardening and landscaping classes for all ages, seasonal farmers' markets, and cultural festivals.

Guadalupe River Park

San Carlos Street and Almaden Avenue

This big, open park is used primarily for celebrations and festivals, such as the 4th of July "America Festival." Otherwise, it's always open for outdoor fun, but if you come for a picnic, bring a blanket; there are no tables.

Kelley Park

1300 Senter Road. Park Hours: 8 am until one-half hour after sunset.
Japanese Friendship Gardens: 10am until sunset. Parking $3, Happy
Hollow Park and Zoo $3 for all ages; San Jose Historical Museum,
$4 Adults, $3 Seniors, $2 Children 4-17. ✱ *277-4191*

Sprawling over 156 green acres in the northern end of San Jose, Kelley Park offers a real variety for your young adventurers, including

Happy Hollow Amusement Park and Zoo, San Jose Historic Museum and the Japanese Friendship Gardens.

Happy Hollow 295-8383

Younger children will love the assortment of play equipment and rides here, including a mini-roller coaster. The zoo features more than 150 different animals, many on the endangered list. Hands-on displays give kids a chance to interact with some of the park's creatures, like a walk-through aviary filled with colorful birds from around the world, or a goat arena where you can purchase food to hand-feed the small goats.

San Jose Historical Museum 287-2290

This historic site at the south end of Kelley Park is separate from Happy Hollow and charges a separate entrance fee. Step back in time and get a glimpse of San Jose at the turn of the century. Among the many restored buildings that have been relocated to this site are an ice cream and candy store (where you can buy a real treat), a bank, a bandstand, and a post office. Ride through town on the vintage trolley car or explore the many fascinating old buildings. Guided tours are available on a drop-in basis. Year-round special events include: Victorian Christmas held the second week in December, Living History Days, held the last weekend in June, and the Civil War Memorial held over Memorial Day weekend.

Louis Pellier Nursery (site of)

Northwest corner of W. St. James/Terraine Sts., Pellier Park

In 1850, Louis Pellier established "City Gardens," a nursery where he and his brothers grew the French prune they introduced into California, which eventually made the Santa Clara Valley famous. The park recognizes Pellier's contribution with plantings of prunes, pears, grapes and other orchard crops.

Plaza de Cesar Chavez

Market Street between San Fernando and San Carlos

This little park nestled in the center of downtown San Jose, across from the Fairmont Hotel, is the site of many local cultural celebrations, including street fairs, parades, cook-offs, arts and crafts fairs, and the famous "Christmas In The Park" (see Chapter 6, Festivals and Special Events). In the warmer months, your kids will enjoy running through the fountains that rise from ground level and really cool off a summer day.

❋ Neighborhood Parks with Playgrounds

Neighborhood parks are usually "just around the block," they often have pleasant picnic areas, they're always free — and those listed here have tot-lots (playgrounds with equipment) for the younger set. For a complete list of city parks in your area, you can contact your local Parks and Recreation Department.

Alviso Park – Wilson Way and School
Backest Park – 13th and Empire
Biebrach Park – Delmas and Virginia
Bramhall Park – Willow and Camino Ramon
Butcher Park – Camden and Ross
Columbus Park – Spring and Taylor
Dana Rock Outcroppings – Houndshaven at Valleyhaven
Hillview Park – Adrian and Ocala
Houge Park – Jackson at Barrett
Kirk Park – Brianwood and Foxworthy
Lone Hill Park – Michon and Vitner
Los Paseos Park – Avenida Grande and Via Vista
Ramblewood Park – Kinsule at Dundale
River Glen Park – Bird and Pine
Roosevelt Park – Santa Clara and 21st
Ryland Park – San Oedri and 1st near Fox
Solari Park – Cas and Arboles
Starbird Park – Boynton and Williams
Watson Park – East Jackson and 22nd

❋ Gardens

Who doesn't long for a tranquil place now and then to relax and re-charge those over-stressed batteries? Gardens can fill that need in your life. And no one is too young or too old to enjoy the beauty and calm of these lovely places.

Hakone Japanese Gardens

21000 Bog Basin Way at Springer Av., Saratoga. M-F, 10-5; weekends 11-5. ❋ *771-4494*

For a quiet, relaxing stroll, amble along pathways lined with waterfalls, streams and fish-filled ponds. The Cultural Exchange Center, often the site of special events and weddings, has a tea museum. Designed in 1918 by a Court Gardener to the Emperor of Japan, these gardens were laid out in the style of a 17th-century Zen garden. The effect can be quite calming.

Overfelt Gardens

McKee Road and Educational Park Drive. Open daily from 10 am until sunset. Free. ✸ 277-5277

On land donated by the Overfelt family, one of San Jose's founding families, you can enjoy a variety of attractions: a wildlife sanctuary with a number of species of birds, water creatures, the Chinese Cultural Garden, a Fragrance Garden for the visually impaired and a self-guided arboreal trail. Not the place to come if the kids need to burn off some energy; the idea here is to walk, relax, observe, and enjoy the garden's fragrance and tranquility.

Japanese Friendship Gardens

In Kelley Park, 1300 Senter Road. Open 10am until sunset. Parking $3. ✸ 297-0778

This beautiful garden, modeled after Korakuen Park in Japan, symbolizes the relationship between San Jose and its sister city, Okayama, Japan. Not only are the gardens beautiful but the kids will enjoy feeding the exotic Koi fish in the pond (food can be purchased at two feeding stations in the garden).

Municipal Rose Garden

Naglee and Dana Avenues. Open 8 am to one-half hour before sunset. ✸ 277-5435

The Rose Garden was set aside in 1927 to be used for the display of an assortment of over 3,500 rose shrubs with 189 varieties. A detailed map explains the locations of the different roses, which are arranged around a two-tiered water fountain.

✸ Hiking Trails

The San Jose Parks and Recreation Department is very active in developing and preserving regional trails for hiking, biking (in some cases) and enjoying nature. A few of these parks are still in the planning stages and at this time are still undeveloped. When complete, the following trails will cover over 150 miles throughout the area. Many of them will eventually join together to form the Bay Trail (described below) and the Ridge Trail, which will encircle the Bay Area via the surrounding mountains (see Ch. 2, On the Horizon). For more information on the individual trails you can contact the Trail Center, 4898 El Camino Real #205, Los Altos, CA 94022 (415) 968-7065.

Bay Trail *(Undeveloped)*

Will eventually run from Dixon Landing Road in Fremont to Sunnyvale Baylands Park. Hike or bike around the bay.

Coyote Creek Trail *(Partially Developed)*

Goes from Heller Road near Highway 101 south to Bernal Road. It will ultimately extend from Anderson Lake County Reservoir, near Morgan Hill in the south, to San Francisco Bay in the north. Length: 32 miles.

Guadalupe River Trail *(Undeveloped)*

This trail will eventually go from the Bay Trail in the north to Lake Almaden in the south.

Los Alamitos/Calero Creek Park *(Partially Developed)*

Begins at Lake Almaden (Almaden Expressway at Camden in South San Jose) and continues south to Santa Teresa County Park. Length is approximately 6 miles.

Los Gatos Creek Trail *(Partially Developed)*

This trail will eventually begin at the Lexington Reservoir in the Santa Cruz foothills and continue along Los Gatos Creek and beyond into downtown San Jose. Today the developed portion runs from Roberts Road (In Los Gatos) and continues to Leigh Avenue in San Jose. The completed portion is 3.5 miles.

Penitencia Creek Trail *(Partially Developed)*

The developed portion is from Toyon Avenue and runs west to Jackson Avenue. The developed trail is 6 miles long. It will eventually run from Alum Rock Park to the Coyote Creek Trail.

Silver Creek Trail *(Undeveloped)*

This will be a 6-mile trail from the intersection of King and Yerba Buena Roads running southeast to the intersection of Silver Creek and San Felipe Roads.

Thompson Creek Trail *(Undeveloped)*

Located in the Evergreen area, this trail will begin at the intersection of White and Aborn Roads and run south to the end of Silver Creek at San Felipe Road. It will eventually be 7 miles long.

 # County and Regional Parks

If your explorers are ready for more freedom to explore and more wide open spaces, then pack a picnic and head for one of these parks. Any one of them can easily be a whole-day excursion.

Alum Rock Park (see Chapter 1)

Garin & Dry Creek Pioneer Regional Parks

Entrance at the east end of Garin Av., Hayward. (Seasonal parking fee) ☀ *(510) 636-1684*

These two adjoining parks offer a variety of attractions, like a fishing pond, the Red Barn Visitor Center, an Indian grinding rock, and picnic areas.

Calero Park

Almaden Expressway south to Harry Rd. Go rt. on Harry; left onto McKean Rd. Open year-round, 8 to-1/2 hr. after sunset. Fee. ☀ *268-3883*

Former Maalan Ohlone Indian site and once part of El Pueblo of San Jose. Migratory birds, wildflower displays, wildlife.

Coyote Hellyer County Park

Hellyer Av. exit off Hwy 101. Open year-round, 8-sunset. ☀ *225-0225*

Look for waterfowl, foxes, rabbits, wild pigs, turkeys. A velodrome (training site for cyclists, but not open to the public) is on site.

Coyote Hills Regional Park

Thornton Av. exit from Hwy 84; drive north on Paseo Padre Pkwy; turn left on Patterson Ranch Rd.

A preserved wetland that showcases the Ohlone Indian's way of life. Visitor Center with nature store, shellmounds, marsh boardwalk, Bay View Trail, paved loop trail for hiking/bicycle riding. Picnicking areas.

Lake Cunningham Park

South White Road. Open weekdays 6:30 am until one-half hour after sunset; weekends 8 am until one-half hour after sunset. Parking $3; various fees for paddle boats, canoes, rowboats and sailboats. ✳ *277-4319*

The lake, nearly 50 acres by itself, is surrounded by over 200 acres of open space complete with par course, bike trails, jogging course, a dozen or more picnic areas, barbecues, horseshoes, and volleyball courts (bring your own equipment). Water activities include paddle boating, canoeing, rowing and sailing (all boats available for rent daily during the summer; weekend rental available in spring). The little fishermen in your family can also enjoy fishing in these stocked waters. (No extra charge for this but all local laws and licensing do apply).

Next to Lake Cunningham you'll find Raging Waters, another day's adventure in itself (see Chapter 1).

Deer Hollow

In Rancho San Antonio County Park. From I-280 take Foothill Expwy west to first light (Cristo Rey); turn right to the park. Park inside and walk a little more than a mile to Deer Hollow. Open T-Sun 8 to Dusk. Animals are put out by 9 am. ✳ *867-3654*

Part of 900-acre Rancho San Antonio County Park, Deer Hollow is a working farm and environmental education center. Not a petting zoo; these animals are observed from a distance.

 Before you go hiking in California, be sure everyone in your group is aware of the necessary precautions:

✳ Stay on marked trails and avoid touching unfamiliar plants; poison oak is common, and very unpleasant.

✳ Rattlesnakes are a fact of the California countryside, and they're most active during warm months. Although timid by nature, they will strike when unintentionally provoked. Watch where you step, don't overturn rocks (they like to sleep underneath), and never put your hand in a spot you can't see (watch for toddlers, whose curiosity drives them to reach into every hole they see).

✳ Always remember that California's dry, summer grasses are excellent tinder; any spark can set off a fire that can quickly become a disaster. Be sure you know park rules concerning barbecues and campfires.

✳ And it's always a good idea to carry water; it's dry hiking out here, and the strong sun can cause dehydration. A hat will help, too.

Happy, safe hiking!

Elkus Ranch (UC Cooperative Extension)

1450 Purisima Creek Rd., Half Moon Bay ✸ *(415) 726-3148*

Hands-on children's programs in farm and wildland ecology throughout the year.

Joseph D. Grant Park

On Mt. Hamilton Rd. Take Hwy 101 or 680 to Alum Rock Av. Eastbound; turn rt. on Mt. Hamilton Rd., go 8 miles to park. Fee. ✸ *274-6121*

Wildflowers, hiking, mountain bikes on designated trails. The road that leads to this park continues up to the Lick Observatory (see Ch. 2, Planetariums and Observatories).

Hidden Villa/Duveneck Ranch

Los Altos Hills ✸ *949-8660*

A 1600-acre organic farm and wilderness preserve. Hidden Villa offers hands-on, innovative programs promoting environmental awareness and multi-cultural understanding. Farm tours.

Highlands County Park

8500 Highway 9, Ben Lomond ✸ *454-2777*

Besides its huge playground, Highlands has nature trails and picnic areas. Parking fee in summer.

Ed R. Levin Park

From I-680/880, take Calaveras Rd. exit, Milpitas. Drive east on Calaveras Rd. to park entrance. Open 8-1/2 hour after sunset, year-round. Fee. ✸ *262-6980*

Over 64 known bird species have been sighted at this park, which also has wilderness trails. Maybe you or your little bird-watcher will sight a new one.

McClellan Ranch Park

22221 McClellan Rd., Cupertino. Hwy 85 South to McClellan Rd. Take McClellan almost to Foothill Bd. Park is on right side on McClellan. Open 8-to 1 hr. after sunset. ✸ *(408) 253-2060*

A horse ranch during the 1930s and '40s, this 18-acre park has the appearance of a working ranch. Preserved on the property are the original ranch house, milk barn, livestock barn and two relocated historic buildings: Baer's Blacksmith Shop and an old water tower. Also at McClellan Ranch are corrals (where Rolling Hills 4-H Club members raise rabbits, chickens, sheep, pigs and cattle), and a Junior Nature Museum featuring small live animal exhibits and information about indigenous bird, animal and plant species.

Mount Madonna Park

Hwy 152 (Hecker Pass Hwy), 10 mi. west of Gilroy, on Pole Line Rd. From east, use Hwy 101; take Hwy 152 West exit. Fee. ✻ 842-2341

Visitor center; fishing pond; 1/2 mile, self-guided nature trail; view white fallow deer. Free slide shows in amphitheater each Sat., Memorial Day-Labor Day.

New Almaden County Park

I-280 East to Vine St. exit; turn right onto Vine St., and continue until it becomes the Almaden Expressway. Continue past intersection of Almaden Expressway and Camden Av. to Almaden Rd, on right. Follow Almaden Rd. for 2.5 miles to center of town.

New Almaden was the site of North America's first and richest quicksilver mine, from 1847-1912. The entire village of New Almaden is a historic landmark of restored homes and community buildings. Surrounding hills are full of tunnels, one open to visitors. Visit the New Almaden Museum, behind the Clayton House.

Ohlone Regional Wilderness/Wilderness Trail

Accessible only via the Ohlone Wilderness Trail by hiking or horseback, the area offers backpack camping and outstanding vistas. Wildlife includes golden eagles, mountain lions, bobcats and tule elk. Some of the East Bay's most remote and beautiful wilderness areas are accessible through the Wilderness Trail. Permit required.

Pinto Lake County Park

757 Green Valley Rd., Watsonville. Fees. ✻ 454-2777

Spring-fed lake, hiking trails, bird sanctuary.

Quail Hollow Ranch and Regional Park

800 Quail Hollow Rd., Ben Lomon. Open Memorial Day-Labor Day. ✻ 454-2777

300-acre ranch with hiking trails; home to several endangered plant species. You can park in the lot and walk about a mile to Deer Hollow, a 10-acre working farm and environmental education center (see above).

San Benito County Historical Park

8300 Airline Hwy., Hollister. $3 park fee for use of picnic grounds. Open daily, 8-5:30. ✹ *628-3312*

Picnic facilities/4 barbecue pits in a 33-acre setting that includes historic buildings (home, dance hall, barn) from the Hollister area. Structures are under restoration and not yet open as of this printing.

Sanborn-Skyline Park

Near Hwy 9, two miles west of Saratoga. Turn south onto Sanborn and go 1 mile to entrance ✹ *867-6940*

Miles of hiking trails, Youth Science Institute, 867-6940; Sanborn American Youth Hostel (AYH).

Saratoga Springs

22801 Big Basin Wy., Saratoga. Near Hwy 9, about 2 miles west of Saratoga Village. ✹ *867-3016*

This 120-acre resort in the Santa Cruz mountains is the site of one of the first mills on Saratoga Creek. Remnants of the mill remain. The creek and redwood forest make a stunning backdrop for picnics.

Stevens Creek Park and Upper Stevens Creek Park

From Cupertino, take I-280 to Foothill Expressway. Follow Foothill Bd. 3 miles west to park's northern entrance ✹ *867-3654 and 867-9959*

One of most popular birding parks in the Bay Area, with 125 species recorded. Horse rentals. Bobcats, foxes, and mountain lions have all been seen here. The park's sloping topography offers views of pristine hillsides and the Santa Cruz Mountains. Reservoir Trail leads to Laurel Flat Trail, which connects with Fremont Open Space. Carry water and pack snacks. Trail guides available at the park office, off Stevens Canyon Rd.

Sulphur Creek Nature Center

1801 D St., Hayward. Free. ✹ *(510) 881-6747*

Wildlife education and rehabilitation center, part of the Hayward

Area Recreation & Park District. Live indigenous mammal displays, pet lending, nature programs, special events.

Sunnyvale Baylands

999 E. Caribbean Dr., at intersection of Lawrence Expressway and Hwy 237, Sunnyvale. Open 8-5:30, Nov-April; 8-8:30, May-Oct.; $3/ vehicle; no charge for walk-ins. No pets; wheelchair accessible. ✳ *730-7709*

72 acres of grassy areas include picnic facilities, amphitheater, 4 playgrounds and walking paths. Views of 105 acres of wetlands from pathways.

Sunol Regional Wilderness

Geary Rd. off Calaveras Rd., six miles south of I-680.

Naturalist programs at the Old Green Barn on wildlife, Indian heritage and pioneer history.

Uvas Canyon County Park

✳ *779-9232*

One-mile nature trail follows Swanson Creek to several waterfalls, which are best seen in late winter/early spring.

Vasona Lake Park

298 Garden Hill Dr., Los Gatos. Open 8-sunset; $3 per car. ✳ *356-2729*

A large park with lots to do: picnic areas scattered throughout the park, boats for rent, attractions like the Wild Cat Railroad, a merry-go-round and two playgrounds. Kite-flying spaces, and bring bread to feed the large population of ducks and other waterfowl. Los Gatos Creek Trail meanders through the park. Site of the Youth Science Institute (YSI), 356-4945.

✸ Reserves and Preserves

Reserves are areas in which certain flora, fauna, wildlife are protected. In Preserves, hunting is permitted.

Año Nuevo State Reserve

Rt. 1, south of Half Moon Bay ✳ *Tel: 1-800-444-PARK*

Guided interpretive walks into the Northern Elephant Seal rookery,

Dec-March. 2½-hour walks are 3 miles long; reservations/tickets required. Self-guided walks to view seals, April 1-Nov. 30; permits issued on first-come, first-served basis through 3:30 pm daily.

Arastradero Preserve

Arastradero Rd., Palo Alto. Open 8-to-sunset. ✳ *(415)329-2423*

Mixture of rolling savanna grassland and evergreen forest. Arastradero Lake, open for fishing, 6½ miles of trails. Nature programs.

Elkhorn Slough National Estuarine Research Reserve

1700 Elkhorn Rd., Watsonville. Hwy 1 to Moss Landing; take Dolan Rd. to Elkhorn Rd. Open 9-5, W-Sun ✳ *782-2822*

Mingling of fresh/salt waters creates a rich environment for abundant wildlife in the 1,400-acre estuary park. Visitors center, bookstore and displays. Weekend guided tours.

Lighthouse Point and Field

West Cliff Dr., Santa Cruz ✳ *429-3777*

Stroll along the cliffs of this 35-acre park while looking for feeding birds on rocks below.

Mission Peak Regional Preserve

Reached either via Stanford Avenue or from the parking lot of Ohlone College in Fremont.

The preserve offers hiking/riding trails and outstanding vistas through beautiful wilderness areas.

Pescadero Marsh Natural Preserve

Hwy 1, Pescadero ✳ *(415) 879-0832*

One of few remaining original California Coastal Marshes, and a major migratory stop (for birds) along the Pacific Flyway. Three trails; Pescadero Bridge is best for bird watching. Docent-led tours.

Schwann Lagoon

East Cliff Dr., near Twin Lakes Beach, Santa Cruz ✳ *688-3241*

Canoe or kayak into the lagoon, which is a wild bird refuge.

State Parks

California is a state enriched by an abundance of State parks, many found within a days' drive of San Jose. Check for special events throughout the year. Information: (916) 653-6995.

Big Basin Redwoods State Park

21600 Big Basin Wy., Boulder Creek. 9 miles northwest of Boulder Creek on Big Basin Wy. (Hwy 236) ✳ *(408) 338-6132 or (800) 444-7275*

Oldest park in the California State Park system. Hike, bike, or stroll along more than 50 miles of redwoods that are more than 2,000 years old. Guided walks available during summer. Dogs on leash allowed in some areas; day-use fee.

Burleigh-Murray State Park

Higgins-Purisima Rd.,just south of Half Moon Bay.

A one-mile hike along Mills Creek takes you to the ruins of an 1850s dairy barn.

Butano State Park

In the Santa Cruz Mountains, five miles south of Pescadero on Cloverdale Rd. ✳ *879-0173*

Bicycle trails, view of Año Nuevo island.

Castle Rock State Park

15000 Skyline Bd., (2/5 miles southeast of Saratoga Gap), Los Gatos. Open daily, 6 to sunset. No dogs. ✳ *867-2952*

Over 3,600 acres of semi-wilderness, including some spectacular views, rolling meadows, waterfalls, shady forests. Hiking/horse trails, picnic areas, caves.

Henry W. Coe State Park

Near Morgan Hill. Hwy 101 to Morgan Hill; go east on Dunne Av. ✳ *779-2728*

Visitor center/museum, hiking trails, wildflower walks offered at 1pm each Sunday, March-May. Longer Sat. hikes at 10am, evening programs, 8pm. Annual Wilderness Weekend in late April (call for details).

Henry Cowell Redwoods State Park

5 miles n. of Santa Cruz on Graham Hill Rd. From Hwy 1, Santa Cruz, take Hwy 9 north towards Felton. Park entrance 5.5 miles from Hwy 1 ✳ *438-2396*

Easy nature trail hike through redwood grove; interpretive center.

Fall Creek State Park

Felton-Empire Rd. (.6 miles west of Hwy 9), Felton ✳ *688-3241*

Primitive area with over 10 miles of scenic trails, some of which take you past lime kilns which fired limestone for cement during the 1800s.

Forest of Nisene Marks State Park

101 Madeline Dr., Aptos. Trailhead located on Aptos Creek Rd., two miles from Soquel Av. ✳ *429-2850*

Some of the trails through this forested wilderness on Aptos Creek take you to the ruins of a logging camp, an intriguing find during your hike. Plaque on trail commemorates the epicenter of the 1989 Loma Prieta earthquake, which measured 7.1 on the Richter scale.

Fremont Peak (see Ch. 2, Planetariums & Observatories)

On San Juan Canyon Rd., 11 miles from San Juan Bautista ✳ *623-4255*

244 acres; includes observatory.

Portola State Park

Portola State Park Rd., La Honda, six miles off Hwy 35 ✳ *(415) 948-9098*

Hiking trails, and one of the tallest trees in the Santa Cruz Mountains.

San Juan Bautista State Historic Park

On Star Rt. 156, seven miles west of Hollister ✳ *623-4881*

Mission town includes hotel and historic buildings including Mission San Juan Bautista, founded in 1797 (see Ch. 8, Missions & Adobes).

Santa Cruz Mission State Historic Park

126 High St., Santa Cruz ✳ *425-5849*

Includes replica of the 12th California mission and the Neary-

Rodriquez Adobe, built in 1791. The adobe is one block off the plaza on School Street (see Ch. 8, Missions & Adobes).

Wilder Ranch State Park

On Coast Rd., off Hwy 1, two miles north of Santa Cruz. Open 10-4 daily ✳ _426-0505_

This theme park, centered around a 19th-century dairy farm, includes restored ranch buildings and a Victorian mansion with period furnishings. Antique farm equipment and cars. Hiking trails, tours.

State Beaches

With an eye on the future, State Beaches preserve our beautiful coast for everyone's enjoyment for generations to come. You can depend on finding a well-managed, well-maintained beach with amenities — the perfect family destination on a hot day; call for specific information.

Half Moon Bay State Beach
✳ (415) 726-6238

Natural Bridges State Beach
✳ 423-4609

View migration of Monarch butterflies (see Ch. 2, Animals).

New Brighton State Beach
✳ (800) 444-7275

Pescadero State Beach
✳ (415) 726-6238

Pompano State Beach
✳ (415) 726-6238

San Gregorio State Beach
✳ (415) 726-6238

Seacliff State Beach, Santa Cruz
✳ 688-3222

✹ Lighthouses

Pigeon Point Lighthouse

Pigeon Point Lighthouse AYH-Hostel, Pescadero. Look for the lighthouse on the west side of Hwy 1, five miles south of the Pescadero Rd. turnoff. ✹ *(415) 879-0633*

The Pigeon Point Lighthouse (also a hostel, or hotel) is located just off California's ocean-hugging Highway One, 50 miles south of San Francisco and 27 miles north of Santa Cruz. One can hardly find a more dramatic seascape than this.

This second tallest lighthouse on the West Coast was built in 1872. Its original Fresnel lens remains in the tower, although today an automated beacon signals passing ships with its 10-second flash pattern. Lighthouse tours on the hour, each Sunday, 11-3, first-come-first-served basis. Tours limited to 15; arrive 20 minutes prior to tour. Call for fee.

Visit nearby Año Nuevo State Reserve, the only mainland breeding colony of the northern elephant seal, or pick any cozy, high spot to scan the horizon for migrating grey whales, December-May (see Ch. 2, Preserves/Reserves and Wildlife). Butano State Park and Big Basin Redwoods State Park, with more than 17,000 acres of redwoods, are nearby.

Point Montara Lighthouse

16th St. and Hwy 1, between Montara and Moss Beach ✹ *(415) 728-7177*

Between Half Moon Bay and San Francisco (a bit beyond the range of this guide, but worth a mention), you'll come to Point Montara Lighthouse Hostel at 16th St. & Hwy 1, Montara. Established as a fog station in 1875, the Point Montara Fog Signal and Light Station became a hostel in 1980.

The lighthouse sits on 40-foot bluffs overlooking the ocean. Although the lighthouse is not open for tours, the grounds are open to the public between 7:30-9:30am and 4:30-9:30pm. You can walk around the lighthouse, or take the small path to a sheltered cove and tidepools.

✹ Panorama Points

The views in the San Jose region range from urban and civilized to breath-taking and wild. Here are some suggestions for unforgettable vistas; don't forget your camera!

Davenport - Whale watching *(Ch. 7, Day Trips)*

Fremont Peak Overlook *(Ch. 7, Day Trips)*

Natural Bridges State Park, Santa Cruz *(Ch. 2, Animals)*
Stroll out to the eucalyptus-shaded, wooden platform to experience swarms of Monarchs during butterfly season, from October-March.

Roaring Camp & Big Trees Railroad *(Ch. 2, Transportation)*
Chug through stands of towering, fragrant redwoods to the summit of Bear Mountain, or across a 1909 steel bridge spanning the granite and sandstone gorge of the San Lorenzo River.

Skyline Boulevard Overlook *(Ch. 7, Day Trips, Santa Cruz to San Mateo)*

Skyline Drive *(Ch. 7, Day Trips)*
Vista overlooking the tree-covered hillsides of Sanborne Skyline County Park and Castle Rock State Park.

Santa Cruz Beach Boardwalk Ferris Wheel *(Ch. 7, Day Trips)*
For a wide-angle view of the Monterey Bay, take a ride on the ferris wheel at the Boardwalk.

Upper Stevens Creek Park *(this chapter)*

4
Performing Arts
for Children

T he lights dim...the hushed murmur fades...Those little bodies that can never sit still, strain for a glimpse of whatever the spectacle has to offer.

What can match the breathless anticipation of those endless few moments before the show starts? Whether it's a puppet show or the Symphony, kids love the drama and the spontaneity of a live performance. A few well-thought-out rules about acceptable behavior at public performances, placed in the appropriate small ears, should ensure their enjoyment of the moment, as well as the enjoyment of those around you. No matter how young, kids like to know what's expected of them.

No one is too young to appreciate the arts. Kids are natural born artists, intimately involved in the arts by instinct — irrepressible actors, singers, dancers — and there's no audience quite as enthusiastic as a young one! So get them ready for their next foray into the world of live entertainment — and their next, and the next... the San Jose region doesn't lack for them.

But shows come and go, and seasonal offerings vary each year. Be sure to check local publications for more information. Check with the San Jose Arena for special performances, like the circus. There are also publications on the campuses of the many colleges that highlight their performances.

Also check with all the Parks & Recreation districts for performances, special classes, summer workshops and other art-related activities for families.

Happy hunting. Break a leg.

DANCE

There are many dance studios around the San Jose/Santa Clara area. Most of them offer regular schedules of performances; some are affiliated with other performances. Some of them are listed here; check the Yellow Pages under Dancing Instruction for more.

✳ American Dance Academy
3001 Ross Av. ✳ *265-0649*

Their performance group, the American Academy of Young Professionals, presents a regular schedule of shows. Classes for age 3 to adult.

✳ San Jose Cleveland Ballet
99 Almaden Bd. ✳ 288-2800

The oldest co-venture in ballet, this troupe shares its artistic staff between the two cities of its name. Its Arts Education Outreach helps bring performances to schoolchildren who otherwise might not have the opportunity to see live ballet. Performances year-round, presenting a well-rounded image of the dance. Season subscriptions available.

✳ San Jose Dance Theatre
753 N. Ninth St., Suite 234 ✳ 293-5665

Home of the San Jose Dance Theatre Ballet Company, they offer a regular schedule of performances and classes in classical ballet, jazz, tap and modern dancing.

✳ Santa Clara Ballet School
3086 El Camino Real, Santa Clara ✳ 247-9178

This official school of the Santa Clara Ballet Company offers classes for age 3½ through adult, as well as regular performances.

MUSIC

✳ American Musical Theatre of San Jose (formerly called the Civic Light Opera)
Center for the Performing Arts ✳ 453-7100

Four productions a year, plus summer classes for kids age 10 and up in performance and the technical aspects of musical theater production. The classes take place at 1717 Technology Drive (near the airport).

Is this music or theater? Yes!

✳ Bell Choirs
This is an unusual musical form where a group of performers ring bells in different tones to produce a memorable, delightful sound. Holiday seasons are a favorite for bell choir performances, but there are concerts throughout the year. The San Jose area has over 100 bell choirs, so

there's quite a selection to choose from; but they're often smaller groups and their performances go unnoticed by the press.

Bell choirs are often affiliated with churches, but there are also community groups and school groups. You can get information about joining one or attending a performance by contacting the churches directly (check the Yellow Pages under Churches), by reading the local publications, or by calling (510) 651-2767. They can tell you more, or give you the current on-line Web address for up-to-date information.

✸ California Youth Symphony

Flint Center, DeAnza College, Cupertino; San Mateo Performing Arts Center ✸ (415) 325-6666

Anyone between the ages of 8 and 18 can play in the Youth Symphony, which is actually three performance groups of varying skill levels. Auditions are held each June. They perform 7 programs throughout the year, and it can be inspiring for your budding musicians to see a symphony performance by people their own age. The most advanced group, the California Youth Symphony Orchestra, tours internationally. These are family-oriented concerts, since most of the musicians have siblings and relatives in the audience, and they sometimes offer free outdoor concerts.

✸ Fremont Symphony Orchestra

Gary Soren Smith Center for the Fine and Performing Arts, Ohlone College, Fremont. To mail ticket requests: P.O. Box 104, Fremont, CA 94537. ✸ (510) 794-1652

31 years in existence at this printing, the Fremont Symphony begins a special program in 1995/1996: Musical Treats for Children, a series of hour-long concerts to educate and delight children 7-12. Their regular season goes from October through May, including one free children's concert in March and a young artists' performance in April.

✸ Hewlett-Packard Symphony Orchestra

4981 Ponderosa Terrace, Campbell CA 95008 ✸ 447-3166

This group is made up mostly of Hewlett-Packard employees, and concerts, although open to the public, are usually small and "in-house."

✸ International Mariachi Festival

Guadalupe Park ✸ (800) 642-8482

Your family can experience live mariachi music plus crafts, food and a Mexican-style market at this annual outdoor celebration.

✳ Peninsula Symphony Orchestra

San Mateo H.S. Performing Arts Center; Flint Center, DeAnza College,
Cupertino. ✳ *(415) 574-0244*

This 47-year-old community orchestra gives 12 performances each year; the one in July is free. This is a reasonably priced opportunity to hear fine music, and once a year they offer a special Family Concert at the Mountain View Center for the Performing Arts; call for up-to-date information.

✳ San Jose Chamber Music Society

Le Petit Trianon Theater, 72 N. 5th Street ✳ *286-5111*

This organization presents chamber music groups to San Jose about 8 times a year. A favorite with families is their holiday brass concert in December, which kids love. Special discounts for kids under 12.

✳ San Jose Jazz Festival

San Jose Museum of Art stage. ✳ *993-3990*

Once a year, jazz takes over at the MoA. Come listen, tap your feet, enjoy!

✳ San Jose Museum of Art's Monthly Concert Series

110 S. Market St. ✳ *294-2787*

On the first Wednesday of every month, at the Museum of Art, you and your family can enjoy music from around the world, from different eras and in different media, from classical quartets to jazz to bebop. Free to museum members.

✳ San Jose Symphony

495 Almaden Bd. ✳ *288-2828*

In the tradition of great music, the Symphony brings the wonder and magic of classical music to San Jose. Several different types of subscriptions are available, as well as a series of outdoor concerts in the summer. Teachers get discounted tickets for their classes, and there's talk of offering family concert series in the future.

If your youngster plays a symphonic instrument and would like experience performing, check into the Symphony's Junior and Senior Youth Orchestras.

Box Office hours: M-F, 10-4; tickets available through BASS ticket outlets and Tower Video/Records.

✹ Silicon Valley Youth Conservatory
San Jose State University ✹ *924-4701*

Although not strictly a performance group, this deserves mention here. Its director, Richard Aldag, hopes to help combat the crisis in music education in public education by offering young people the opportunity to become proficient in instrumental music. Classes are available on a semester basis, with excellent scholarships offered, in just about any kind of music your child could want to try. Musicianship is a skill, an art, and can be a lifelong joy — provided we have the chance to learn it. If your child's school is lacking in music programs, give this group a call.

And more..

Many **churches** offer concerts, large and small, during the year. Not as intimidating as a fancy concert-hall, this can be a non-threatening way to introduce your little ones to fine music. See the Yellow Pages under Churches.

Throughout the year in the San Jose region, **festivals** offer families fun, food — and music. You don't have to travel thousands of miles to hear exotic, ethnic music — just come to the Nikkei Matsuri (Japanese), the Greek Festival, the Chinese Summer Festival or any of the other ethnic festivals in the area. Their music will give you a glimpse of another culture, another way of listening, and you may be pleasantly surprised. See Chapter 6 for a list of regional festivals.

And don't forget to check the performance schedules at the local **colleges and universities.** They offer regular musical performances and often have children's concerts or outdoor concerts where kids can behave like kids and still enjoy the music. See Chapter 10 for a list of colleges and universities in the area.

OPERA

There's nothing quite like this extraordinary combination of music and drama to stir the blood — and no one enjoys a good, colorful spectacle more than children! Everyone can find something unforgettable in a well-presented opera. San Jose offers....

☀ Opera San Jose

2149 Paragon Dr. ☀ 437-4450

The mission of the Opera is to develop young professional talent, and you can see lots of it here. Besides 4 magnificent productions each year, with 11 performances of each production, Opera San Jose also offers a full, rich program for children through their Educational Outreach, which goes to San Jose schools. In these 15-session programs, children can participate in the actual creation of an opera, which they write and perform in. Call the Opera or your local school for information.

☀ San Jose Civic Light Opera

4 N. 2nd Street ☀ 971-1212 and 1717 Technology Dr. ☀ 453-7113

See American Musical Theatre of San Jose, in the "Music" section.

PUPPETS

Children can really identify with these "pretend people" as they confront life's ups and downs. Puppets can be a wonderful teaching tool, a source of entertainment, a way for children to learn how to cope with life's vagaries as they identify with these ingenious little creations. Watch their faces as they watch a performance; it's total involvement.

☀ Happy Hollow Park and Zoo

1300 Senter Rd. ☀ 295-8383

Happy Hollow offers a free puppet show on weekends that can really involve the kids, especially the younger ones. This provides a nice respite during a whole-day visit to the park, or can be a pleasant outing of its own.

☀ Punch's Opera Puppet Theatre

☀ 998-4785

This travelling show, whose performances are rooted in 18th-century European puppet theater tradition, will perform at any event. It's a very interactive show, and will involve the grown-ups as much as the little guys (said to bring out the ham in everyone!). Performances can be tailor-made to suit the occasion.

> *The next time you happen to be on I-80, you might want to plan to stop at **Creative Play Puppets**, 1881 Walters Court, Suite C, Fairfield (707) 428-1828. This is the only felt-puppet factory in the U.S., and they offer a fascinating 5-station tour that shows how puppets are created, from first cut to final product. Takes about 30 minutes; open 9-4 daily; free.*

✹ Snapdragon Puppet Productions
✹ *(415) 578-1725*

Snap the fire-breathing dragon will perform at any function, and is a special favorite at birthday parties. His (Its?) fairy-tales are interactive and involve kids and grown-ups alike.

And if your kids would love to produce their own puppet theater, you can order **Puppet Theater** from World Book Catalog. The kit includes four full-color stage backdrops, scripts, 19 scratch-resistant cardboard puppets and parent's guide. World Book Catalog, Box 182246, Chattanooga TN 37422; (800) 874-0520.

THEATER

Being experts at "let's pretend," children often get quite caught up in a good drama or comedy. There's good theater, and good children's theater, all over the San Jose/Santa Clara area. Some of the entries below feature regular children's theater; some offer the occasional kids' show. Some involve the kids, some are only to watch and enjoy. Call first.

✸ American Musical Theatre of San Jose
(formerly called the **Civic Light Opera**)

See the "Music" section.

✸ California Theater Center
Sunnyvale Community Center Theater, Sunnyvale ✸ *245-2979*

From September to June, they do shows for young audiences, appropriate from pre-school age and up (for school outings or home-school groups). During the summer, they host the San Francisco

Shakespeare Theater for 4-week long sessions which all end in a performance. Introduce your child to the magic of applause and a job well done. Information is available in early March.

✸ Children's Playhouse of San Jose

✸ *578-PLAY (578-7529)*

Founded by a group of teachers who felt that musical theater can benefit kids' skills and self-esteem, the Children's Play House has classes and performances throughout the year, starting at the first-grade level. Various performances throughout the year. One-week summer camp at three different locations (San Jose, Los Gatos and Morgan Hill).

✸ City Lights Theater Company

529 S. 2nd Street ✸ *295-4200*

This small, non-profit theater produces 5 shows per year plus a summer season, all "off-beat and out of the mainstream." Probably not family/kid fare, but when yours are older and their tastes are more sophisticated, this might be a place to keep in mind. During the summer, they also host other multi-cultural theater groups.

✸ Northside Theatre Company

848 E. Williams St. ✸ *288-7820*

A small, professional group that's been together for over 17 years, the NTC runs a "clean" show — they try to gear their performances as much as possible toward a family audience, and they use as much young adult talent as they can. They do school workshops, and sometimes offer summer conservatories; call for up-to-date information.

✸ Palo Alto Children's Theater

1305 Middlefield Rd., Palo Alto 94301 ✸ *Info (415) 329-2216* ✸ *Box office (415) 329-2651 (open 1-6pm,T-Sat)*

This theater, by and for young people, offers performances October through May. In July they begin their summer stock theater, age 8-18, which gives several performances at the end of each session, and a series of summer classes for ages 8-10 and 10-high school.

✸ San Francisco Shakespeare Theater

666-2222; Bay Area Shakespeare Camp (summer) ✸ *(415) 666-2313 or (800) 978-PLAY*

The goal of this group is to bring quality theater to as many people as possible. They accomplish this by bringing Shakespeare's plays to the public, free, throughout the summer, in St. James Park. But a large part of this goal is also accomplished by bringing the magic of the Bard to our children. Summer and fall sessions of Bay Area Shakespeare Camps are offered to youngsters age 8-16. They can learn all aspects of theater arts, as well as performing arts. The Theater also brings Shakespeare to schools; call (415) 666-2310 or (800) 978-PLAY to schedule a performance.

College and university campuses offer a rich selection of cultural experiences all year long; some are specifically tailored for young people, like some of the seasonal offerings (children's Christmas plays, for example, or young people's concerts). Check newspapers and call each location. See Chapter 10 for a list of colleges and universities in the area.

✳ Santa Clara Junior Theater

969 Kiely Bd., Santa Clara, in the middle of Central Park across from Kaiser ✳ *244-7258*

Three or four performances per year, kids performing for kids, and classes all year long beginning at age 4. Your youngsters can learn acting, singing and dancing, and in the summer they offer a special summer conservatory.

✳ San Jose Children's Musical Theater

753 N. 9th Street, Suite 135 ✳ *288-5437*

This is the largest children's theater in the U.S. where kids perform for kids. They offer eight full-scale productions each year, and everyone who auditions gets a part. Classes year-round, and in the summer they offer an intensive 3-week program called the Conservatory of Performing Arts (COPA) where your youngsters can learn voice, drama, dance as well as the variety arts (stage make-up, combat, etc.). Two summer sessions, one in June and one in July/August. Call for locations of classes.

✳ San Jose Repertory Theater

1 N. 1st Street (box office); performances held at the Montgomery Theater, San Carlos & Markets Streets ✳ *291-2255*

This group doesn't normally do children's theater, but some of their plays are right for older children. For the 1995 Christmas season they'll be doing a children's play, so it does occasionally happen; call to check.

5
Sports and Recreation

I f there's one thing that's universal to all children, it's what you'd call the perpetual motion factor. Kids have to MOVE! Whatever other intellectual pursuits they may explore, they need the balance of regular vigorous physical exercise (as do we all) to maintain physical as well as mental health. The ancients knew it; "mens sana in corpore sana" (a sound mind in a sound body) said some old sage who must have had children. And nothing's changed over the centuries, except the technology. Unfortunately, with more and more children spending their free hours watching television or playing video or computer games, the sound body is often not given equal time.

This chapter offers lots of possibilities for finding just the right kind of activity for their little growing bodies, either individually or as a family. There is also a listing of sports that they can watch for inspiration, but the main focus here is what they can DO.

So if you're not already involved in family or individual sports activities on a regular basis, start now with this list. And if you don't find exactly what tickles your family's fancy here, check with the Parks & Recreation districts (see County listings in the white pages of the telephone directory); they offer all kinds of organized activities, classes, workshops, another programs. School districts also offer athletics for the community. San Jose is a great place for outdoor activities, all year round. There's something here for everybody, and you'll have fun picking and choosing.

SPECTATOR SPORTS

✹ MAJOR LEAGUE SPORTS

✹ **Golden State Warriors** (National Basketball Association) play at the Oakland Coliseum, I-880 and Hengenber Road in Oakland. Information: (510) 382-2305. The season starts in November, with 41 home games and a total of 82 games for the season.

✹ **Oakland A's** play in the Oakland Stadium, I-880 and Hengenber Road, Oakland (next to the Oakland Coliseum). Tickets can be purchased by phone at (510) 638-0500. Their season begins in April and ends in October, with a total of 144 games; 72 are home games.

✳ **San Francisco 49ers** (National Football League) play at famous Candlestick Park on the bay, Giants Drive and Gilman Avenue, San Francisco. Ticket information: (415) 468-2249. The Season kicks off in July and ends at the end of December. They play a total of 21 games each season.

✳ **San Jose Sharks**

(National Hockey League) play at the San Jose Arena, West Santa Clara and Autumn Streets, San Jose. Ticket information: (800) 366-4423. The season consists of 41 games beginning in October and running through the end of April.

(SAN JOSE CONVENTION AND VISITORS BUREAU)

✳ **San Jose Rhinos** (Roller Hockey) play in the San Jose Arena, West Santa Clara and Autumn Streets, San Jose. Ticket information: 287-4442. Their season begins in June and ends in August, with a total of 12 home games.

✳ **San Jose Saber Cats** (Arena Football) play in the San Jose Arena, West Santa Clara and Autumn Streets, San Jose. Ticket information: 993-2287. Their season begins in April and ends in August with 7 home games.

✳ **COLLEGIATE SPORTS**

✳ **San Jose State Spartans**. Their basketball team plays at the Events Center Arena, 7th and San Carlos, in San Jose. The football team plays at Spartan Stadium, 7th Street between East Alma and Humbold Streets. For information on either team or tickets call 924-3267.

✳ **Santa Clara University Broncos** basketball team plays at Toso Pavillion, 500 El Camino Real, Santa Clara. Ticket information can be obtained by calling the ticket office at 554-4660.

✳ **Stanford Cardinals**. Basketball games are played in the Roscoe Maples Pavilion, Campus Drive East between Galvez and Serra Streets. Football games are played at Stanford Stadium, Nelson Road off Galvez Street. Tickets can be purchased by calling (415) 723-1021.

❋ Other Sports Events

There are a variety of sports events available in the new San Jose Arena. Call the San Jose Arena Information Line for upcoming events 287-9200. A few of the annual events include major league sports, the circus, figure skating, and ice skating shows.

❋ Racing

San Jose Speedway, located at the Santa Clara County Fairgrounds, 344 Tully Road, San Jose (294-7223). Enjoy Sprint Cars, Late Model Stock Cars, Dwarf race cars, and Mini-Sprints. During the County Fair you can watch the Demolition Derby.

INDIVIDUAL, FAMILY AND TEAM SPORTS

❋ Archery

There are two local ranges in the San Jose area, **Archery World**, 754 the Alameda, (971-9705) and **Trophy Taxidermy & Archery**, 2632 Union Avenue, Campbell (559-3396). Both are indoor facilities where you can rent equipment or bring your own. You can also buy supplies there, and they offer instruction and archery leagues.

❋ Backpacking

For a great place to get started, check out trails in Chapter 3. Another excellent resource for trails for kids in the area is a book called <u>Best Hikes with Children, San Francisco South Bay</u>, by Bill McMillon with Kevin McMillon (see Recommended Reading at the back of the book). To get outfitted, try R.E.I. or Mel Cottons (see Shopping, Chapter 2).

❋ Badminton

Badminton is the perfect family sport, ideal for developing eye-hand coordination and accessible to any age and any budget. The equipment is inexpensive, easily obtainable at most toy stores, and simple to learn. Children of any age can play, simply by adjusting the net level (or not using one). If you don't have your own grassy space to play, it's easy to carry your set to the nearest park, and as you develop more skill, you'll be surprised how physically demanding the game can get!

✳ Ballooning

What child of any age doesn't dream of floating up in the sky — like a balloon? You can either arrange to have your own ballooning adventure or simply go watch someone else have theirs. **The Gentle Adventure** in Morgan Hill (778-1945) or **Balloon for Higher** in Los Gatos (358-0043) can help you arrange it.

✳ Baseball and T-Ball/Batting Practice

In the Yellow Pages under Baseball Clubs and Parks you'll find a list of Little Leagues and places to hone your skills, including schools and batting ranges/cages. Also contact your local city or county Department of Parks and Recreation, your area's religious organizations, school districts and other community organizations to find a team for your child to join.

✳ Basketball

Contact your local city or county Department of Parks and Recreation, your area's religious organizations, YMCAs, school districts and other groups listed in this book or the Telephone Directory, to find a team for your child to join.

✳ Bicycling

Cycling is a great way for the whole family to get lots of exercise and enjoy the scenery at the same time. It's an activity that requires no special skill, and once you have bikes, can be indulged at any time without any strain on the budget. The San Jose area abounds with lovely parks for cycling; you can bike around the neighborhood park, or you can go for miles and miles on one of our many bike trails (see Chapter 3). If you can put your bikes in or on the car, this is the perfect way to see many different sites throughout the bay area.

Unlike most other sports, bicycling has the unique advantage of getting you where you're going, and we could all help reduce the damage to our environment if we used our bikes instead of cars on short errands, to get to work, to school, etc. Be sure to wear helmets, and obey all traffic rules (bikes are considered a vehicle, and are subject to the same rules as all other vehicles).

There are many organized cycling activities throughout the area; most bike shops can provide information on these. You may also want to check with local and Regional Parks and Wilderness areas for organized bike trips. See the Yellow Pages under Bicycles.

✳ Bowling

This is another sport that the whole family can participate in, regardless of skill level. There are many bowling lanes throughout the area, several of which offer leagues for various ages. Many have special bumpers for younger children who are prone to "gutter balls." See Bowling in the Yellow Pages.

✳ Boxing

The San Jose Police Athletic League offers a junior boxing league to the young men in the community. Practices are held at Agnews State Hospital. Call (727-8118) for more information.

✳ Camping

No other family activity is like camping. Nothing quite compares with the experience of waking up all together under the trees or in the primitive desert, to the sound of birds or a nearby creek or the aroma of a pine forest, knowing that you've met nature on her own terms, been kind to her, and enjoyed all that she has to offer.

For many people who enjoy outdoor activities, California and camping are synonymous. Campgrounds are available through California's extensive and beautifully-maintained State Parks system, through various local Parks & Recreation systems, and on private campgrounds. For general information, call (800) 444-7275. For general U.S. Forest Service information, call (415) 705-2874 (San Francisco). See the White Pages under Government listings, Parks and Recreation, for local areas.

✳ Cross-Country (Nordic) Skiing

For families who love winter sports, cross-country skiing can be just what you've been looking for. It's less dangerous than downhill skiing (no speed involved, unless you get into downhill cross-country), much cheaper, and easier to stay in groups. Trails take you through pristine, peaceful scenery, and anyone who can walk can enjoy the sport with little or no training.

You can indulge in cross-country skiing just about anywhere there's snow, but it's probably best to use maintained trails, especially for beginners. If you don't have your own equipment, most large sporting good stores can help get you started or rent you what you need (see Sporting Goods under Shopping in Chapter 2).

The Tahoe region is dotted with ski areas, and most of them offer cross-country trails. The National Forest Service maintains trails in the National Forests; a common destination for Northern California skiers is the El Dorado National Forest (916/645-6048). They also maintain a series of Snow-Park areas where you can leave your car and go enjoy some fun in the snow — sledding, skiing or just building a snowman.

The world's largest cross-country ski touring center is Royal Gorge, off I-80 at the Soda Springs exit. They have trails for all levels of difficulty, a separate area for toddlers, overnight cabins, day touring, ski camping and more. Norden and Kirkwood also attract a lot of Nordic skiers. The Sierra offers spectacular scenery in any season, but to glide silently through its winter mantle of pure snow is an experience that cross-country skiers speak of with awe and reverence. No one is too young for such an experience.

✳ Fencing

Fencing is a sport that has been around for centuries. What child hasn't pretended to do his imaginary enemy in with a jab of his imaginary sword? If your child would like to be a bit more serious and get involved with this age-old sport, you can contact **The Fencing Center**, 40 North 1st Street (298-8230) for fencing instructions. Apparel and equipment can be purchased from **The Fencing Post**, 2543 Monticello Way, Santa Clara (247-3608).

✳ Fishing

There are numerous lakes and stream nearby which are ideal for anglers of any age or skill level. You'll want to check with the California Department of Fish and Game (415) 688-6340, for regulations, limits and season dates. For beginners you might want to start with a local stocked fish pond, where you don't need to wait all day to make your big catch. Contact Fish and Game or a local Sporting Goods store for recommendations.

If sports fishing is more your style, head for the ocean. You can arrange for a family charter with any of a number of charter companies along the coast. Look in the Yellow Pages under "Fishing Parties," for more information or you might want to contact the Santa Cruz or Half Moon Bay Chambers of Commerce to get the name of a reputable charter company (see Chapter 10).

✳ Football

Contact your local city or county Department of Parks and Recreation, you area's religious organization, school districts and other groups listed in this book or in the Telephone Directory, to find a team for your child to join.

✳ Golf

The choice is enormous! There are at least 22 golf courses in the

San Jose area, all within an easy drive. There's even a computerized golf "course" called **Saratoga Indoor Golf Range**, 1080 South Saratoga-Sunnyvale Road, Sunnyvale (446-4653). You can "play" various courses (by hitting the ball into a big computerized screen), hit practice balls and even get your golf swing analyzed by computer. For the younger golf set, there are several Mini-golf areas (see Golf Courses – Miniature in the Yellow Pages) that have arcades and various family fun attractions besides the mini-golf. If your little golfer is more serious than miniature golf but not quite ready for the big courses you can contact any of the local courses to see which provide little golfer clinics. One such course is **Pruneridge Golf Course**, 400 North Saratoga Avenues in Santa Clara (248-4424). They offer a free little golfer's clinic every Saturday.

米 Gymnastics/Tumbling

Gymnastics is one of the best individual sports to help children build coordination, strength, endurance, concentration and self-esteem. There are lots of places in the San Jose area to indulge in the sport, both for children and adults; For a complete listing se the Yellow Pages under Gymnastics Instruction.

米 Hiking and Backpacking

Kids love the adventure of exploring the wilderness, and in the San Jose area there's plenty of it to explore! You can meander along some of the milder, level trails within the city or suburbs, or you can head to the hills for more of a challenge. From flat Baylands to rolling hills to steep, rugged mountain terrain, the San Jose area has it all.

Here are some suggestions of places to go for different types of hikes. Whether your goal is a strenuous hike or a leisurely stroll through nature, you'll find it nearby. First, the easy family walks in or within a short drive of town. (For more information, see Ch. 3, Parks, and Recommended Reading on page 205.)

Coyote Creek Trail. This trail runs from Dixon Landing Road in Fremont to Sunnyvale Baylands Park.

Los Alamitos/Calero Creek Park. Begins at Lake Almaden (Almaden Expressway at Camden Road in South San Jose).

Pentitencia Creek Trail. Begins at Toyon Avenue in San Jose and runs west to Jackson Avenue.

This is just a partial listing, you can explore some more ambitious trails through the Regional and County Parks, and wilderness areas. And check out the Bay Area Ridge Trail (see Chapter 2, On the Horizon).

❋ Hockey

With the recent arrival and popularity of the San Jose Sharks, ice hockey has really taken off in our area. Here are the top locations for kids who would like to get more involved with this sport. The Pacific Hockey League 293-2087 has many different teams which practice in several locations. See Ice Skating, below, for a list of local ice skating rinks.

Running a close second behind Ice Hockey is Roller Hockey. With the development of in-line-skates, this sport's popularity has skyrocketed. **Germic Rollerhockey**, 15349 Los Gatos Boulevard, Los Gatos has both a store (358-1169) and rink (971-2200). You will find all sorts of gear for purchase and rental as well as information on leagues, lessons and birthday parties.

❋ Horseback Riding

Equestrians, junior or otherwise, can indulge their passion at many location throughout the area. A few of the more popular ones are **Garrod Farms Riding Stables**, 22600 Mt. Eden Road, Saratoga (867-9527). They're open seven days a week and offer horse boarding, riding school, horse and pony riding. **Sea Horse & Friendly Acres Ranch** is located off of Hwy 1 at Half Moon Bay, (415/726-2362). They offer beach and coastal trail rides for all ages. **Alum Rock Park Stables**, 16240 Alum Rock Avenue, San Jose

Before you go hiking, here are a few safety precautions that will help make it an enjoyable outing for everyone in the family:

❋ Wear hats. The California sun is famous for a very good reason; the air here is extremely dry, so the sun's rays reach you undeflected by moisture. The weather can get very warm in the summer, and even a mild, flat hike can be unbearable if that strong sun's in your eyes.

❋ Take water bottles – for everyone. The Valley and foothills can be dry and dusty and hiking makes you even thirstier. Kids enjoy the independence and importance of carrying their very own water bottle.

❋ Take mosquito repellent. Although our area is not always known for mosquitoes, they can be a nuisance if you're not prepared. Constant swapping and slapping can make even the tiniest hiker miserable.

❋ Don't move the rocks. Rattlesnakes love to sleep under rocks; never put your hand or foot in a place you can't see. And don't let toddlers or curious little ones reach down any holes in the ground.

❋ Wear solid, sturdy shoes.

(251-8800) offers rides along the many trails throughout Alum Rock Park. All ages are welcome.

For more information and additional listings, see the Yellow Pages under Horse Rentals, Horse Stables and Riding Academies. Some colleges also offer courses in riding. You might also want to check with the Parks & Recreation districts for summer horseback riding lessons.

✳ Ice Skating

You and your whole family can enjoy public skate sessions, or take a lesson at any of the ice rinks in the area. Many of them also offer a  variety of skating supplies, group rates and birthday party packages. **Eastridge Ice Arena** 2190-A Tully Road (238-0440); **Ice Center of San Jose** 1500 South Tenth Street, San Jose (279-6000); **Ice Chalet**, 10123 North Wolf Road, Cupertino (446-2906); **Iceoplex**, 44388 Old Warm Springs Road, Fremont (510/490-6621).

✳ Martial Arts

Karate, Judo and other forms of martial arts develop discipline and awareness of self, respect for others, concentration, strength, forbearance and the ability to focus and concentrate. Instructors emphasize the defensive nature of the art. It's always wise to observe a class first before enrolling your child, and many places offer a free first lesson. You'll find many listing under Martial Arts in the Yellow Pages, and many Parks & Recreation districts offer martial arts classes during the year and throughout the summer.

✳ Ornithology (Bird-Watching)

The Bay Area has the privilege of being on the Pacific Fly-way for migrating birds. There are many outstanding opportunities for bird-watching throughout the year and the area; this list is just the beginning.

San Francisco Bay National Wildlife Refuge, near Dumbarton Bridge and Highway 84 (415/792-3178)

Hayward Shoreline Interpretive Center, 4901 Breakwater Avenue, Hayward (510/881-6751)

Lucy Evans Bayland Interpretive Center, 2775 Embarcadero Road, Palo Alto (415/321-2111)

Villa Montalvo, 15400 Montalvo Road, Saratoga (741-3421)

You can also check with Regional Parks and Wilderness areas as well as local park districts for organized bird-watching opportunities.

Rock climbing trains the mind and the body, and now you can do it indoors.

✳ Rock Climbing (Mountaineering)

There are three great training facilities in our area that simulate the rock climbing experience without the element of danger that exists with real rock climbing. They call these facilities "climbing gymnasiums." These can be a great place for kids to let off steam while training their bodies and minds. **Planet Granite**, 2901 Mead Avenue, Santa Clara (727-2777), is the world's largest. With over 15,000 square feet and 70 ropes (to rappel from). You and the kids can get a lesson, rent shoes and harnesses, then set off to climb and rappel as long as you like. **Pacific Edge**, 104 Bronson #12, Santa Cruz (454-9254) is the second largest with 13,000 square feet. They also rent the ropes, harnesses, shoes, and offer lessons. Finally there's **City Rock**, 1250 45th Street Emeryville, (510/654-2510). They offer individual and group lessons, and will rent all of the same gear as the other two facilities.

✳ Roller Skating

Skating develops coordination and balance, keeps you fit and it's a sport the whole family can do together with minimum drain on the pocketbook. There are several rinks listed in the Yellow Pages under Skating Rinks, most of which offer instruction and provide the skates. Many also sell miscellaneous skate equipment. Since the latest craze is in-line-skating, many locations will let you bring your own; however, they are subject to inspection.

✳ Running and Track

A regular regimen of physical exercise is necessary for a sound body — and what could be easier than just putting on your running shoes and hitting the track, or the park, or the street? There are jogging tracks in many of San Jose's parks; call Parks & Recreation for your area. Most colleges and local schools have a track that's open to the public when there's no meet or other event happening. And many Parks Districts offer Track during their summer sessions.

✳ Shooting/Pistol & Rifle Ranges

This is a sport that is alive and well here in the Wild West! San Jose and the surrounding area has several shooting ranges where people can practice firing handguns and rifles. Look in the Yellow Pages under Rifle and Pistol Ranges.

✳ Skiing (Downhill)

The Sierra Nevada mountain range is one of the most popular in the world, and we are fortunate to be within a few hours of it. The Sierra offers skiing for novice to expert, in areas scattered from southern to northern California.

The South Lake Tahoe area is one of the most accessible from here. Downhill and cross-country ski equipment can be purchased or rented at most of the sporting goods stores in the Sacramento area, and you can get information about ski centers there, too. For general information, check the Yellow Pages under "Ski Resorts and Arrangements" or "Skiing Equipment;" also try South Lake Tahoe Visitors Authority (916/554-5050 or 800/AT-TAHOE), or the South Lake Tahoe Chamber of Commerce (916/541-5255). Many sporting-goods stores offer ski-trip packages, as do some of the colleges; also contact Parks & Recreation Districts for possible ski packages.

✳ Snow Parks

Snow Parks provide access to many of the Sierra's best winter recreation areas for cross-country skiing, snowmobiling, sledding, snowball-throwing and any other snow fun you can think of. Permits are available at outdoor specialty stores, various resorts, ranger stations and business in the Sierra; and the California State Automobile Association district offices. Season pass by mail at Permit Sales, SnoPark Program, P.O. Box 942896, Sacramento 94296-0001. Call first for up-to-date prices: (916/653-8569).

❋ Snowshoeing and Snow Camping

Snowshoeing is a unique way to see some spectacular unspoiled scenery and get lots of exercise. It requires little preparation other than general physical conditioning, and there's no age limit, young or old. Snow-camping can be the experience of a lifetime — providing you're hardy enough!

Eagle Mountain Nordic has snow-shoe trails; it's about one hour east of Sacramento on I-80, at the Yuba Gap exit (916/783-4558). R.E.I. Sports at 20640 Homestead Road, Cupertino (446-1991) can give you some tips on snow camping.

❋ Soccer

In recent years, the popularity of soccer has soared all across our country. It's offered at many recreation centers, community centers and churches, and many youth groups also have teams. For general information, see the Yellow Pages under Soccer Clubs, or call one of the sporting-goods stores; see the Yellow Pages under Sporting Goods – Dealers. **Off The Wall Soccer**, 700 Mathew Street, Santa Clara (988-6900) offers year- round soccer leagues, and most Parks and Recreation Districts offer soccer camps.

❋ Special Olympics

The Special Olympics of Santa Clara County is very active, and they can put you in touch with area coordinators and events. This is also a great event to volunteer for either as individuals or as a family. For information, contact their office at 1530 Blossom Hill Road, San Jose (267-2734).

❋ Swimming and Aquatics

Swimming is the best exercise; no other sport tones all the muscles in the body quite like it. Whether you take your swimming seriously or you just like playing in or near the water, the San Jose area is awash with possibilities!

There are dozens of pools in the area; see the Yellow Pages under "Swimming Pools – Private" (where you may need to be a member to participate) and "Swimming Pools – Public" (a fee may be required but no monthly or annual membership). During the summer months, most of the Parks & Recreation Districts have swimming and aquatics classes, for babies through adults, as does the YMCA. The community colleges offer youth swim classes during the summer as well.

✳ Tennis

Much like badminton, but bigger, and still a sport that any family can enjoy. All you need is a racket and a few fuzzy balls, and you're ready to head for one of the many public and private tennis clubs or courts around the area. See the Yellow Pages under "Tennis Clubs – Private", "Tennis Courts – Public" or "Tennis Instruction." Many Parks & Recreation Districts also offer summer tennis instruction for all ages.

✳ Sports Camps

It would be impossible to list all of the summer sports camps available in the San Jose area. This is outdoor paradise — if there's a sport you can do outdoors, you can find a camp for it here, for any age or level.

School districts offer summer sports programs; Parks & Recreation Districts have sports training for the summer (see Chapter 10 under Summer Classes). Most of the local papers print an annual section on summer camps as does <u>Bay Area Parent Magazine</u>, a free local newspaper for parents. Also check with community centers, community colleges, and local libraries for additional offerings.

✳ Youth Centers and Organizations

Many Community Centers around the area have sports, educational and social programs for young people. For information and locations of these centers, see Chapter 10, Special Assistance Telephone Numbers, or contact the local Parks & Recreation Districts. Some churches also have youth centers.

San Jose also has many youth organizations where your child can learn life skills, enjoy social programs, engage in sports and outdoor activities, learn about science, art and generally have fun growing up. Some of these include:

Camp Fire Boys and Girls, 1600 Coleman Avenue, Santa Clara (988-6969)

Boy Scouts of America, 970 Julian Street, San Jose (280-5088)

Girl Scouts, 1310 South Bascom Avenue, San Jose (287-4170)

Junior Achievement of Santa Clara County, 5201 Great America Parkway, Santa Clara (988-8915)

YMCA, 1190 Emory Street, San Jose (298-3888)

YWCA, 4343 Leigh Avenue, San Jose (269-7534)

6
Festivals and Special Events

No matter what the season, there's always something happening somewhere in the San Jose/Santa Clara region. Many of these events are local; many take place in what's loosely termed "the greater Santa Clara Valley region." But then, the five counties covered in this book — Santa Clara, San Benito, San Mateo, Alameda and Santa Cruz — are all neighbors, and what's a few miles between neighbors?... especially if the goal is to have a good time!

All of the events listed are open to the public; some charge, some are free. But keep in mind that things change; don't be too disappointed if the event you picked isn't happening this year. There's surely another one to take its place, to add to your list of favorites. Check the local newspapers for more up-to-the-minute happenings, too, since special events and sponsors come and go. You can also call the local Convention & Visitors Bureau (see Chapter 10 for numbers). You'll undoubtedly find things to add to this list — but this should get you started.

Festivals are in San Jose unless otherwise specified.

☀ JANUARY

❋ **East-West Shrine Football Game**, Stanford University Stadium, Stanford. Annual all-star college game to benefit Shriners hospitals for crippled children. (415) 661-0291

❋ **Golden Gate Doll Show**, Santa Clara County Fairgrounds. Even if dolls aren't your little ones' cup of tea, this show is fascinating, offering every imaginable type of doll from antiques to computer-generated cuties. 494-3100

❋ **Sealabration**, Año Nuevo State Reserve, south of Half Moon Bay. Proceeds from this special tour among the elephant seals go to the San Mateo Coast Natural History Association. With any luck you'll see some newborns, or hear the males trumpeting. (415) 879-2025

❋ **Tet Festival**, Santa Clara County Fairgrounds. Help ring in the Vietnamese New Year at this Southeast Asian festival featuring culture, food, arts and crafts. 494-3100

☀ FEBRUARY

❋ **Gem and Mineral Show**, Santa Clara County Fairgrounds. What kid doesn't like collecting rocks? Here they can learn more about gems and rocks than you've ever forgotten. 494-3100

❋ **Monarch Butterfly Migration Festival**, Natural Bridges State Beach, Santa Cruz. Once a year, beautiful fluttering orange butterflies swarm to the Santa Cruz area. They're only here a few days, so plan ahead. Experience the wonder of walking among thousands of the lovely creatures. Tours, festival, music and food, too. 423-4609 (Natural Bridges), or 425-1234 (Santa Cruz Visitors' Bureau).

❋ **Santa Clara Valley Kennel Club Dog Show**, Santa Clara County Fairgrounds. Kids and dogs, dogs and kids — the perfect combination! If you're thinking of getting a dog, or just love looking, you'll see them all here. 494-3100

❋ **Valentine's Fun-Run**, Pruneyard Shopping Center, near Campbell Park, Campbell. Run/walk together, or just show the kids your stamina, at the 10K fun-run and 5K walk sponsored by the city of Campbell the Saturday before Valentine's Day. Rain or Shine. 866-2105

MARCH

❋ **Computer Swap Meet**, Santa Clara County Fairgrounds. Where else but in the heart of the Silicon Valley? Bring your little experts and come explore new and used computer equipment. 494-3100

❋ **Full Moon Prowl**, Del Valle Regional Park. A full-moon prowl through the wilderness at night, when lots of critters are up and about. Register in advance; for ages 8 and up. (510) 373-0332 (Del Valle Park) or (510) 862-2244 (Sunol-Ohlone Regional Wilderness).

❋ **Great Train Robberies**, Roaring Camp & Big Trees Railroad. Historic re-enactment of famous California lawmen and desperados, including shoot-outs, train robberies and other mayhem. 335-4400

❋ **Irish Week Celebration**. The San Jose/Dublin Sister City Committee celebrates Irish culture with two weeks of activities throughout the San Jose area. 225-9626

❋ **Mercury News 10K Race & 5K Walk and Fitness Expo**, Guadalupe River Park. Information and vendors' exhibitions. Make family fitness fun! 920-5672

❋ **Sports & Fitness Expo**, San Jose McEnery Convention Center. Come find out what's happening in the world of health, fitness and sports. Kids under 12 get in free with a paying adult. Fashion shows, demos, hands-on activities, lots of very physical things to do, like trampolines, gymnastics, skating, even indoor rock-climbing. March and October. 286-5600

☀ APRIL

☀ **Cherry Blossom Festival**, Memorial Park, Cupertino. Japanese cultural festival featuring music, dance, arts and traditions. 777-3200

☀ **Children's Fair**. Celebrate the Month of the Young Child (a nationwide celebration) at this family event. Free activities, games and entertainment for kids 2-10. Also health screening and community information. 277-2617

☀ **Community Flea Market**, Community Center, Milpitas. Who knows what treasures await your little collectors here? 942-2470

☀ **Coyote Kids**, Coyote Hills Regional Park, Fremont. A day camp where your kids can explore the marshes of the East Bay, learning about the natural region and how the local indigenous people survived here. (510) 795-9385

☀ **Earth Day Every Day**, Plaza de Cesar Chavez and the Civic Auditorium. Celebrate the environment and Arbor Day with entertainment, exhibits, food and family fun. Most events free. 277-5208

☀ **Easter Egg Hunt**. Various attractions throughout the San Jose region have these, usually accompanied by other festivities, like petting zoos, train or pony rides, prizes, etc. Call the attraction (see Index).

☀ **Film & Video Festival**, San Jose State University Student Union. Film screenings and seminars, for older kids who love movies. 924-6263

☀ **KAZA's Children's Dance & Lip Sync Contest**, Mexico Theatre, 1191 Santa Clara St. Kids ages 5-13 get a chance to ham it up imitating their favorite musical performer. 984-1290 or 575-1290

☀ **March of Dimes Annual WalkAmerica**, Lake Cunningham Park. The largest walking event and annual fund raiser for birth defects in the nation. A cause all parents can relate to. 271-4747

☀ **National Library Week**, various branches. Special programs; contact your local branch (see Chapter 2, Libraries). 277-4874

☀ **Rock Climbing Basics**, Sunol-Ohlone Regional Wilderness. Teenagers (and older) can learn the basics of rock climbing, like safety, tying knots, belaying, rappelling and more. Also in August. (510) 862-2244

✳ **Spring Carnival**, Community Center, Campbell. Rides, games, booths, entertainment. 866-2105

MAY

✳ **American Folk Arts Festival**, San Jose Civic Auditorium. (707) 778-6300

✳ **Antique Fly-in Air Show**, Watsonville Municipal Airport, Watsonville. The thrill of over 500 antique planes, both in the air (several air shows Saturday and Sunday) and on the ground. 496-9559

✳ **Arts & Crafts & Music Festival**, Casa de Fruta, 6680 Pacheco Pass Hwy., Hollister. More than 100 vendors of hand-made crafts exhibit pottery, leather-work, crochet, stained glass, dolls and more. Also live entertainment and lots of food. Free. 842-9316

The San Jose Historical Museum recreates historic events using authentic costumes and props.

✳ **Cinco de Mayo**, Almaden Bd., between San Carlos and Santa Clara Streets. Five stages of live Hispanic international talent. (Other Cinco de Mayo celebrations in the region; check publications, college campuses, etc.) 258-0663 or 292-5197

✳ **Civil War Memorial**, San Jose Historical Museum, 1600 Senter Rd. Your young historians can imagine they're really in 1863, with all the costumed participants. 287-2290

✳ **DeAnza Day**, DeAnza College, Cupertino. Hot-air balloon rides are among the festivities at this gala festival. 864-8756

✸ **Festa d'Italia**, Hecker Pass, Gilroy. Music, dancing, culture and food, food, food! 842-2121

✸ **Gold Rush Days Extravaganza**, Roaring Camp, Felton. Step back in time to the era of the Gold Rush for some rip-roarin' family fun. 335-4400

✸ **Happy Hollow Park & Zoo Art Show**, 1300 Senter Rd. 295-8383

✸ **Human Race 10K Run & 5K Walk**. Pancake breakfast and various festivities are part of this race day that benefits all non-profit organizations in Santa Clara County. 247-1136

✸ **KAZA's Children's Dance & Lip Sync Contest**, second part of the competitions (see April). 984-1290 or 575-1290

✸ **Long Board Invitational**, Steamers Lane, Santa Cruz. Surfers and surfboards by the hundreds. 684-1551

✸ **Mother's Day celebrations** at various attractions throughout the San Jose region.

✸ **Mushroom Mardi Gras**. Morgan Hill. Food, fun, entertainment, and a MunchkinLand and petting zoo for the kids. 779-9444

✸ **National Historic Preservation Week**. Tours, lectures, exhibits vary. 947-8025

✸ **Native American Pow-Wow Red Road Celebration**, Casa de Fruta, 6680 Pacheco Pass Hwy., Hollister. Tribes from the U.S., Canada and Mexico gather to celebrate their culture, dance, and foods. 842-9316

✸ **Nikkei Matsuri**, Fifth & Jackson Streets. Japanese Arts & Craft Faire; crafts, dance, drummers, exhibits and food. 241-0900 or 298-4303

✸ **Paramount's Great America Memorial Day Celebration**, Great America Parkway, Santa Clara. 988-1776

✸ **Pow-wow**, Stanford. Intertribal celebration of Native American cultures; food, arts & crafts, activities. (415) 723-4078

✸ **Prune Festival Wine and Arts**, the Pruneyard, Campbell. Music, crafts, food and lots of kid-stuff — Astro-jumping, trampolines, clowns, face-painting, etc. 378-6252

✸ **Rainbow Singers Spring Concert**, Community Center, Milpitas. Kids between 4 and 14 perform for the public after each session of youth chorus classes (approx. May, August and December). Come inspire your budding singers. 942-2470

❋ **Rubber Stamp Festival**, Civic Auditorium in Parkside exhibit hall, Market St. Thousands of rubber stamps, accessories, supplies, demos and prizes. Is there a kid who doesn't love rubber stamps? 272-0211

❋ **Sunnyvale Hands on the Arts**, Sunnyvale. Over 50 different hands-on art programs to choose from. Be creative. 730-7343

 # JUNE

❋ **Arts & Crafts & Music Festival**, Casa de Fruta. (See May) 842-9316

❋ **Avenue of the Arts**, Willow Glen District. Strolling entertainers, food booths, arts & crafts. 298-2100

❋ **Classic Summer Memories**, Christmas Hill Park, Gilroy. Classic cars, dancing, food and more. 848-7733

❋ **Father's Day Rail Enthusiast Day**, Roaring Camp & Big Trees Railroad, Felton. Dad gets treated to all kinds of privileges today, like a free engineer's cap or a ride in the cab of the locomotive. 335-4400

❋ **Gymnastics Invitational (Budget Rent-a-Car)**, San Jose Arena. One of the world's premier gymnastics events. Tickets at the Arena, or from BASS ticket centers. 287-9200

❋ **Happy Hollow Park & Zoo Animal Birthday Celebration**, Happy Hollow Zoo. 295-8383

❋ **Highland Games**, Community Center, Campbell. Pageantry, color and family fun at this Scottish event. Highland sports, crafts, bagpipes and other music, dancing and lots of food. Special family tickets. 225-3305

❋ **Hoop-it-Up 3 on 3 Basketball**, Almaden Bd. Ages 10-60, male, female or wheelchair division. 370-9262

❋ **Japanese Cultural Fair**, Mission Plaza, Santa Cruz. One of Santa Cruz County's oldest ethnic groups celebrates its culture. 429-3778

❋ **Juneteenth Festival**, San Jose State University. Celebrate the achievements of African-Americans in the areas of film, literature, music, dance, drama and others. 292-3157

❋ **Living History Days**, San Jose Historical Museum, 1600 Senter Rd. (Kelley Park) Take the family back in time, for some old-fashioned fun. 287-2290

✳ **San Jose Doll Show & Sale**, Santa Clara County Fairgrounds. Dolls of every shape and size, to admire or take home. Furniture, clothes, etc. (415) 459-1998 or 494-3100

✳ **San Jose Greek Festival**, St. Nicholas Greek Orthodox Church. Music, food, dancing, family fun. 246-2770

✳ **San Jose International Triathlon**, Lake Cunningham. Swim, bike, run, or just come for the pre-triathlon events. 866-8848

✳ **San Jose Public Library Summer Reading Club**. Promotes independent reading for pleasure. Contact your local branch. 277-4874

✳ **Strawberry Festival**, Los Gatos Civic Center, 110 E. Main St. Lots of family fun, to benefit physically and emotionally abused children. 379-3790

✳ **Sunset Dinners**, Mirassou Vineyards. 274-4000

✳ **Take Daddy to See a Mummy**, Rosicrucian Park (Egyptian Museum). 947-3636

☀ JULY

✳ **Armenian Picnic**, Naperdac Hall & Park, Montague Expwy. An ethnic celebration filled with music, food and entertainment. 257-6743

✳ **Chinese Summer Festival**, San Jose Historical Museum. 287-2290

✳ **Firefighters Chili Cook-off**. Milpitas. 295-6999

✳ **Fourth of July Car Show**, near City Hall, Campbell. Kids'll get a kick out of these old roadsters. 866-2105

✳ **Fourth of July Celebrations**. Just about every area has one; this list will get you started in the San Jose area. See Chapter 10 for a list of Chambers of Commerce and Visitors Bureaus for the region.
Mirassou Vineyard, 274-4000, ext. 268
Municipal Stadium, San Jose 297-1435
Paramount's Great America, Santa Clara 988-1776

✳ **Gilroy Garlic Festival**, Christmas Hill Park, Gilroy. This is the biggie. You don't need to like garlic to have a great time here! See Chapter 2, On the Horizon, for the future of garlic in Gilroy. 842-1625

✳ **International Mariachi Festival**, Guadalupe River Park. Several stages of mariachi music, shopping at a Mexican-style market, crafts and food. Games and toys for kids. 292-5197

✳ **Jumpin' Frog Contest**, Roaring Camp & Big Trees Railroad, Felton. Bring a frog or rent one. Winners go to the Jumping Frog Jubilee in Calaveras, where Mark Twain attended just such an event — and wrote about it. 335-4400

✳ **Obon Festival**, Buddhist Church, 639 N. 5th St. Japanese cultural festival. 293-9292

✳ **Rod and Classic Car Show**, Hecker Pass near Gilroy. 842-2121

✳ **San Jose America Festival**, Guadalupe River Park. San Jose's 4th of July celebration. 295-2265, Ext. 483

✳ **Santa Clara County Fair**, S.C. County Fairgrounds. 494-3100

✳ **Tahiti Fête**, San Jose State University Events Center. 266-6579 (Polynesian Cultural Association)

☀ AUGUST

✳ **All American Art & Wine Festival**, Cambrian Park Plaza (last weekend in August). Kids are king here — pony rides, petting zoo, clowns and more. 378-7862

✳ **Country Festival**, Civic Center Plaza, Cupertino. Pony rides, train rides, arts and crafts and activities in a country atmosphere. 252-7054

✳ **Cupertino Art & Country Festival**. Location varies; call. Art and wine for the adults, lots of entertainment and activities for the kids. 252-7054

✳ **Daruma Folk Festival**. Japanese-American cultural event. 298-4303

✳ **Hispanic Cultural Festival**, Christmas Hill Park, Gilroy. Arts & crafts, music, food, dancing. 848-5780

✳ **Rainbow Singers Summer Concert**, Community Center, Milpitas. (see May) 942-2470

✳ **Rock Climbing Basics**, Sunol-Ohlone Regional Wilderness. Teenagers (and older) can learn the basics of rock climbing, like safety, tying knots, belaying, rappelling and more. Also in April; see also "Mountaineering", Chapter 5. (510) 862-2244

❊ **San Jose Jazz Festival**, San Jose Museum of Art stage. Jazz Hotline 993-3990

❊ **Zucchini Festival**. Hayward. Your kids don't eat the stuff? You'll all have fun anyway. (510) 581-4364

SEPTEMBER

❊ **Art in the Park**, Memorial Park, Cupertino. Introduce your kids to fine art the fun way — outdoors. 777-3120

❊ **Celebrate Saratoga!** All over the city. Nine days of festivities — music, food, a parade, dancing and activities. Something for everyone. 867-0753

❊ **Cupertino Community Parade**, Stevens Creek Bd., Cupertino. You don't need to be from here to catch the spirit. 777-3120

❊ **Indian Summer Festival and Pow-wow**, location varies; call. A Native-American celebration, with food, art and traditional dress. 971-9622

❊ **Mexican Independence Day**, Almaden Bd. Parade, food, crafts and several stages with live entertainment. 923-1646

❊ **Santa Clara Art & Wine Festival**, Central Park, Santa Clara. 984-3257

❊ **Tapestry and Talent Festival of the Arts**, Park Av. and Almaden Bd. Ten stages feature live entertainment at San Jose's biggest festival. 293-9727 or 293-9728

❊ **Young Artists Faire**, Community Center, Milpitas. Live entertainment is the backdrop for all the hands-on art workshops and activities for kids. 942-2470 (Deaf callers, 262-3081 TDD)

OCTOBER

❊ **Community Parade**, Cupertino. An old-fashioned parade with uniforms, bands and community spirit. 777-3120

❊ **Fall Festival**, Cardoza Park, Milpitas. Kids will have a ball — pony rides, pumpkin-carving, scarecrow-building contest, petting zoo, magic show, even a costume parade. 942-2470 (Deaf callers, 262-3081TDD)

✳ **Halloween at the Winchester Mystery House**.
What could be spookier than a flashlight tour? 247-2000

✳ **Halloween Ghost Train**, Roaring Camp, Felton.
(335-4484)

✳ **Harvest Festival**, San Jose Convention Center. Artisans fill the Center with their handi-
work, displayed in an early American village
setting, along with entertainment. Not for
very small children. (707) 778-6300

✳ **Italian-American Cultural Festival**, Santa Clara County Fairgrounds. Take the kids to Italy — wander through the re-created Italian
village — play, eat, dance, enjoy! 494-3100

✳ **Milpitas Main Street USA Parade**. Come celebrate cultural diversity. 942-2470 (Deaf callers, 262-3081TDD)

✳ **Monarch Butterfly Day**, Natural Bridges State Beach. The eucalyptus trees here serve as the winter home for these beautiful orange
butterflies that arrive in great numbers in October. 425-1234 or (800)
833-3494 (Santa Cruz Visitors' Bureau)

✳ **Oktoberfest**, Cupertino Village Shopping Center. 253-3355

✳ **Rubber Stamp Festival**. (see May) 272-0211

✳ **Santa Clara Parade of Champions**. Information after July 1st.
246-9190

✳ **Sports & Fitness Expo**, San Jose McEnery Convention Center (see
March). 286-5600

✳ **Willow Glen Founder's Day**, Willow Glen District. A family-
oriented street festival complete with a 10K run, food, entertainment, a
parade and more. 298-2100

✳ **World's Largest Haunted House**, Santa Clara County Fairgrounds.
Is it really? The ghosts and goblins aren't telling! 494-3100

NOVEMBER

✳ **Dickens Faire**, Cupertino Village, Cupertino. A theme festival with
arts and crafts, food, and caroling by costumed groups. 733-6147

✳ Holiday Crafts Fairs. Many areas have them; check with the local Chamber of Commerce or Visitors Bureau (see Chapter 10 for list) or local malls and shopping centers.

✳ Mountain Man Rendezvous, Roaring Camp, Felton. 335-4400

✳ Santa Clara County Holiday Faire and Christmas Lane Show, Santa Clara County Fairgrounds. 494-3100

✳ DECEMBER

(SAN JOSE CONVENTION AND VISITORS BUREAU)

✳ Breakfast with Santa. Many communities have one; check with the Chambers or Visitors Bureaus listed in Chapter 10.

✳ Christmas Pow-wow, call for location. Christmas dinner, Native American-style, with drums, dancing, and singing. 971-9622

A white Christmas at the Plaza de Cesar Chavez (Plaza Park). Are you sure it doesn't snow in San Jose?

✳ Christmas Tree Lighting Ceremony. Many communities have one; check with the local Chamber of Commerce or Visitors Bureau (see Chapter 10).

✳ Holiday Gift Fair and Tree Lighting Ceremony, Community Center, Milpitas. Free child care at this family event that includes arts, crafts, entertainment and more. 942-2470 (Deaf callers, 262-3081TDD)

✳ Messiah Sing-Along, Center for the Performing Arts. What would this season be without the Messiah? This is your whole family's chance to join their voices with those of the Symphonic Choir, accompanied by the Symphony. 246-1160

✳ Pioneer Christmas, Roaring Camp, Felton. 335-4400

✳ Rainbow Singers Christmas Concert, Community Center, Milpitas. (see May) 942-2470

✳ Victorian Christmas, San Jose Historical Museum, Kelley Park. Celebrate the season in a turn-of-the-century atmosphere. 287-2290

EXTENDED EVENTS

JUNE-AUGUST

✳ **Pavilion Summer Concert Series.** Free outdoor concerts in the Pavilion food court. 286-2076

✳ **San Jose Shakespeare Festival.** Six weekend performances of Shakespeare, free in St. James Park. (415) 666-2222

✳ **Santa Cruz Beach Boardwalk 1907 Nights.** On Mondays and Tuesdays, after 5pm, all rides, hot dogs, candy apples, cotton candy and Pepsi cost only 50 cents (1907 prices). 423-5590

✳ **Santa Cruz Beach Boardwalk Pepsi Discount Nights.** On Wednesdays and Thursdays, a specially marked Pepsi can will get you an unlimited ride pass for big savings. 423-5590

✳ **Santa Cruz Beach Boardwalk Summertime Summer Nights.** Free band concerts will take you back to the 50s and 60s. 423-5590

REGIONAL FESTIVALS

Check the list of Chambers of Commerce, Convention and Visitors Bureaus or Visitor Information Centers in Chapter 10 for local information on things like free outdoor summer concerts. You can also contact the California Office of Tourism (916/322-1396) for information regarding the many festivals that take place all year long throughout northern California.

7

Day Trips

S an Jose is a hub for day trips in every direction. To the east lies the Livermore Valley with its parks and open spaces that offer myriad recreational opportunities. A trip south opens the possibility of exploring California mission history, or hiking the trails through a national monument park.

Head west to the redwood forests and the ocean and spend the day riding a historic railway, or frolicking at the West Coast's only remaining beach boardwalk. Turn north to discover the small beaches and beach communities that lie along the Santa Cruz and San Mateo County coasts, including Pescadero, Davenport and San Gregorio.

Along each route you can choose scenic drives, pull off the road and enjoy the view, or visit less-known sites that are certain to be memorable for kids and grown-ups alike. The main criterion, though, when travelling with children is time. Kids don't want to spend the day in the car; they want to DO THINGS. The trips outlined here are an easy drive there and back in one day, with time for lots of things to do once you get there.

And, of course, the better prepared you are, the more smoothly the trip will go. Be sure you have sun hats and sturdy walking shoes, and enough water bottles for everyone — California's a hot, dry place, and even though these destinations are equipped with all the amenities, you'll save lots of time and be able to see and do a lot more if you don't have to keep stopping to find a drinking fountain or a store.

Get yourself a good map. And once you get the hang of it, you'll soon be digging up your own special places to explore. Whatever your family's requirements are for fun, there's lots of it within a day's drive of San Jose!

✳ Fremont/Mission San José Area

From San Jose, take I-680 north to Fremont (about 15 miles).

The recent history of the Fremont area began in the mid-18th century, when Franciscan fathers came to establish a series of self-sustaining villages called missions. Mission San Jose, the 14th of the missions, was constructed in 1797 (see Chapter 8, Missions & Adobes).

Life revolved around the mission until secularization, which brought a new era of livestock ranching and divided the mission's lands into ranchos. Time was unkind to much of the adobe church and other mission buildings, helped along by a series of natural disasters including an earthquake and several fires. But by the turn of the 19th century, most of the mission and the town was rebuilt.

Today, Mission San Jose is a historic district. Its historic buildings include the reconstructed mission, a museum housed in the only remaining original building, and a series of intriguing buildings, from stunning Victorians to a former barber shop and a hotel (now a bed and breakfast inn). Details and histories of the structures are contained in a self-guided walking tour brochure available from the Chamber of Commerce (see Chambers of Commerce list in Chapter 10).

Artesian springs attracted throngs of visitors to the area in the 1800s, and since the well water is as good for grapes as it is for people, wineries sprang up throughout the region. Governor Leland Stanford built what is now the Weibel Champagne Vineyards Winery in 1869 on the site of a former artesian spring resort, at 1250 Stanford Av., just off I-680.

If your family enjoys movies, old or new, you'll want to stop at Niles. Before World War I, Niles was the home of Essanay Studios. Early notable films produced in Niles included most of Bronco Billy Anderson's westerns and Charlie Chaplin's "Little Tramp," where the legendary Chaplin walk was conceived (see Chapter 2, Movie Trivia).

While in Niles, take the gang for a ride on the Niles Canyon Railway, the first and third Sundays of the month, 10-4; (510) 862-9063 (see Chapter 2, Transportation). Niles became an important spot when the railway line through Niles Canyon was completed in 1869, linking the San Francisco Bay Area with the rest of the transcontinental railroad. The original depot, slated for demolition in 1981, was moved to Mission Bd. in Fremont, and is now the home of the Tri-city Society of Model Engineers. The depot is open on the first weekend of each month from 10-4.

On the main street of Niles (Hwy 84), you'll see a sign for the Pleasanton Ridge Regional Area, where you can spend a whole day enjoying whatever outdoor pursuits your family prefers (see Chapter 3, Parks).

Other nearby spots worth investigating:

* Ardenwood Historic Farm, (510) 796-0663, where kids can see what farm life was like from 1870 to the 1920s.
* Coyote Hills Regional Park, with its several-thousand-year-old shell mounds and a reconstructed Native American village (see Chapter 3).
* Shinn Historical Park, including a stop at the Vallejo Adobe, once owned by Don José de Jesús Vallejo, chief administrator for Mission San Jose between 1836-43.

✳ Half Moon Bay

First known as San Benito, today's Half Moon Bay is on a crescent bay of the same name, whose corners project into the Pacific Ocean.

Since nearby Pillar Point Harbor has the only boat-launching site between San Francisco and Santa Cruz, it's a busy place. And with some of the most productive fishing grounds along California's coastline, it's common to see a fleet of commercial fishing boats anchored here.

In the early 1870s, lumber, grain and cattle were the mainstays of tiny San Benito. Today, the town is known for its agriculture, flower production — and pumpkins. Each October, the Art & Pumpkin Festival attracts thousands of people, who enjoy activities like its famous pumpkin carving contest, a parade, and contest for all kinds of pumpkin "mosts" (biggest, heaviest, best carved, etc.).

The approach to Half Moon Bay along Hwy 92 takes you through fields of flowers (in season), Christmas tree farms, and nurseries. The coastal climate allows moisture-loving species like azaleas and rhododendrons to flourish, which can make a springtime visit spectacularly colorful. You'll also pass Obester Winery, which is open for tasting on weekends.

About a mile before Half Moon Bay, you'll pass Spanishtown Center, one of California's first "art only" buildings. Each shop in the center exhibits arts and crafts by area artists, as well as antiques. Just before you reach Main Street, you'll pass what's known as Graveyard Hill. The adjoining cemeteries, enclosed by grayed wooden fence and ringed by gnarled cypress trees, contain graves of the area's pioneer settlers.

Turn left on Main Street, across Pilarcitos Creek, and pick up a walking tour brochure at the Chamber of Commerce, 520 Kelly St., (415) 726-8381, as well as their other publication, "Coastside Trails," which describes nine nearby areas that offer hiking, picnicking, bike trails and horseback riding. Whatever you choose to do, allow time to stroll through downtown — and be ready for fog, which can roll in any time. This is the California coast, complete with its screeching gulls, salty breezes — and ubiquitous fog.

On Main St., stick-style Victorians rub shoulders with Art Deco buildings. Some of the historic structures include the Estanislao Zaballa House, 326 Main (built in 1863), the 1905 Mosconi Hotel at 356 Main, and the Debenedetti Building with its unusual second story bay window. The Cunha Country Grocery, on Main and Kelly offers a chance to step back in time. The Arleta Park Railroad Station, Poplar St. and Railroad Av. (now a private home) is a reminder of the turn-of-the-century time when the Ocean Shore Railway ran between San Francisco and Half Moon Bay.

When you've finished wandering through town, drive down to the harbor to watch the fisherman, both commercial and individual, at work (maybe the anglers in your family can pick up some pointers).

Then go taste the fruits of their labors in any of a number of harborside restaurants that offer the freshest seafood daily.

Several local companies operate whale watching expeditions, in season, and fishing excursion that last for a day or overnight. You can also fish from the pier.

✳ The areas surrounding Half Moon Bay offer nearly every type of outdoor activities; contact the local Chamber for complete information.

✳ Pinnacles National Monument

Near Paicines, southeast of Hollister 389-4485. Route 101 south past Gilroy to Route 25 toward Hollister. Follow Rte. 25 south for 25 miles to Rte. 146 exit south to South 146 turnoff, marked as the park's entrance. Open 24-hours, year-round. $4/vehicle for up to 1 week. Camping: $10/site/day. Pets only in picnic areas and parking lots. No bikes on trails.

Pinnacles is a relatively undiscovered gem. There are several reason for its lack of tourist traffic — it's remote, and it really heats up during the summer. But whatever the reason, Pinnacles is one of the least visited national parks. Which, of course, makes it an ideal place to head for with the kids. Spring and fall are the best times; it's not too hot, and spring wildflowers can be spectacular.

Once part of an active volcano, the angular, craggy mountainsides of Pinnacles rise from 500 to 1,200 feet above the valley. Formed some 23 million years ago when molten rock was spewed over the ground, Pinnacles offers both challenging climbs and more relaxed, family nature walks. If your kids are older (or very active and sturdy), don't miss exploring the two sets of talus (jumbled rock) caves. It's a long hike to the cave mouth, and you need a flashlight once you get there —which makes it all more of an adventure! And don't forget that in caves, the temperature is always the same: cold. Actually, it's cool (in the 60s), but the difference between the caves and the baking trail outside can make it feel even colder than it is, so put sweatshirts in those backpacks (even though the kids will tell you you're crazy as you start out in the heat).

At ground level, you have lots to choose from: 32 miles of hiking trails and 12 miles of wilderness trails. One suggestion is Bear Gulch Trail, a forested trail that skirts Bear Gulch Creek. You can reach it from the trailhead near the Visitor Center or from the Lower Chalone parking area; the kids can keep track of the six bridges in between. As you walk, keep at least one eye up: Pinnacles is a prime bird-watching area. You're sure to see some raptors (birds of prey); if you're lucky you might get a glimpse of Prairie Falcons, American Kestrels, Red-Tailed and Cooper's Hawks, or maybe even experience the thrill of seeing a Peregrine Falcon or a Golden Eagle soaring.

Be sure to pack comfortable shoes (hiking boots are best), a hat, camera/binoculars, and water. There are no water stops along the trail, and it's hot, dry hiking, so be sure to bring enough. If you go through your supplies before you even begin walking, you can purchase bottled water before entering the park, or at the small visitor center/museum. Maps are available at both east and west entrances to the park as well as at several visitor centers.

✳ While you are in the area, you might want to consider continuing south on Hwy 101 to **Soledad**, site of the 13th California mission. See Chapter 8, Missions & Adobes, for information and directions.

✳ San Jose/Salinas/Santa Cruz

Load 'em up and head on south, for lots of different possible combinations of stops for family fun. The first part of the trip down Hwy 101 takes you alongside the foothills of the Diablo Range (to your left). You're heading down toward Salinas, the "nation's salad bowl."

The first town of any size you'll come to is Morgan Hill, named for Hiram Morgan Hill. Take the Business 101 exit to the quaint downtown, which underwent a major facelift in the late 1980s. You can get a sense of the town's early days as you pass the clapboard United Methodist Church, Monterey at Fourth St., built in 1893. If you want to delve a little deeper into the past, stop in at the Morgan Hill History Museum, which was Hiram Morgan Hills' home, on Main Avenue.

Each year in late May, Morgan Hill celebrates its largest crop, mushrooms. If you plan your trip to coincide with this, be sure to plan extra time, either to enjoy the Mushroom Festival or to deal with the extra traffic while driving past. This event can draw about 50,000 people; it's jam-packed with food, fun and activities — but the roads can get pretty congested.

If you leave town on 101, you'll soon come to the road that goes off to the left up to Henry W. Coe State Park (see Chapter 3, Parks). This can be a whole-day or overnight (camping) destination, so you might want to save this stop for another day.

Continue down Business 101 (Monterey St.), through the little town of San Martin to Gilroy. There are hills on both sides of you as you go through and beyond Morgan Hill; if you get here at just the right time in the spring, you can enjoy the remarkable sight of hillside after hillside covered with brilliant golden poppies (California's other gold), the state flower of California.

As you enter town, you'll read on the signs that Gilroy is the Garlic Capital of the World. Gilroy produces the majority of the country's garlic, and in late July the town turns out to celebrate that distinction. On your way through town you'll pass the "History of Garlic" mural, but remember (especially if you have finicky eaters): you don't have to like garlic to have a great time at the festival. If you want a sense of this community, visit the memento-packed museum on Fifth St. (see Chapter 1, Museums), and if you happen by on a Thursday, stop in at the Farmers' Market. (Many different crops are grown locally, and you'll pass a variety of fruit and veggie stands along 101 and the major roads.)

Depending on the time you have, you might want to head east after Gilroy on Hwy 152, to Casa de Fruta Orchard Resort, outside of Hollister. This is a blend of campground/resort, picnic ground, country store, restaurant and petting zoo; it could well be a whole day's excursion, or it makes a perfect lunch-and-browsing stop mid-way on your tour.

From Casa de Fruta, head south on Hwy 156 to Hollister, the San Benito County seat. Hollister's downtown was listed on the National Register of Historic Places in 1993. Architectural styles, many with European influences, range from Italianate to Greek Revival to Mediterranean Revival. Stop by at the San Benito County Historical Museum, on Briggs Alley, for a slice of local history, or treat the kids to some of the area's bounties at the Friday Farmers Market on 7th and San Benito.

From Hollister you can continue on Hwy 156 west toward San Juan Bautista (see Chapter 8, Missions). At this point, you have three choices: you can take Hwy 156 to 101, where you can return north to San Jose or you can turn south to Salinas through Prunedale. You can take the San Juan Grade/Salinas Rd. from San Juan Bautista to Salinas. Or, if you're still up for adventure, you can take the 11-mile drive up the mountain to Fremont Peak State Park before continuing to Salinas.

The drive up to Fremont Peak (named for explorer John C. Fremont, who first planted the American flag there) is not for the faint-of-heart. It's one of those roads your kids will talk about for years — extremely narrow (often barely wide enough for two vehicles to pass), and for the last three to four miles (the Peak is at approximately 3,200 ft.), there are no guardrails. If you or your kids suffer from car-sickness or fear of heights, this might not be the place for you.

But the panoramas along the Gabilan Mountain Range can be spectacular, especially in wet years, when the wildflowers will astound you. And if you're learning about the stars, you'll want to visit the "observatory" —the telescope located on the peak. Astronomy programs, scheduled throughout the year, include viewing. If you plan to take in a star show, you might want to look into a campsite for the night; this road is challenging enough in daylight —I wouldn't want have to drive it at night.

If you decide to take the San Juan Grade, know that it, too, is a two-lane road, though a fairly straight one except as it leaves San Juan Bautista, and has some unpaved stretches. And it, too, offers panoramic vistas along the way.

Salinas is Steinbeck country, where the Pulitzer Prize-winning writer spent his childhood, and developed many of his plots. If you cruise Old Town you'll pass the Steinbeck Library and the Steinbeck House, where you can have lunch amidst Steinbeck memorabilia.

While in Salinas, you can absorb a little history at the Boronda Adobe, Boronda Rd. and W. Laurel Dr. (see Ch. 8, Missions & Adobes), and at the Harvey-Baker House (see Ch. 2, Museums).

From here, head northeast on Hwy 183 to Castroville, known as "The Artichoke Center of the World," and on to Moss Landing and Elkhorn Slough. At Moss Landing, Hwy 183 becomes Hwy 1. It skirts Watsonville, where summer fruits — strawberries, olallieberries (similar to boysenberries) and raspberries — can be picked at local farms. If time permits, drive into downtown and stop at the William H. Volck Museum (see Ch. 2, Museums).

From Watsonville it's a pleasant drive northwest along Hwy 1 to Santa Cruz. Along the last stretch of highway, you have a choice of artsy, beachside communities to dally in, like Rio del Mar, Aptos and Capitola.

✳ San Juan Bautista

Hwy 101 south, past Morgan Hill; look for the exit to San Juan Bautista, near Gilroy. San Juan Bautista State Historic Park, 623-4881. Mission San Juan Bautista, 623-4528. Entrance to State Historic Park: Ages 13 and over, $2; 6-12, $1, under 6, free. Open daily, 10-4, except major holidays. Mission open daily for Mass at 8:30 a.m. Mission gift shop and museum open March 1-Oct. 31, 9:30-5; Nov-Feb, 9:30-4:30 623-4528. For specific events, dates and times: San Juan Bautista Chamber of Commerce 623-2454.

San Juan Bautista is the largest and most well-preserved of the original missions, yet has little of the commercial trappings of other mission towns. The original frontier mission, founded by Fray Fermin Lasuén in 1797, was owned by the King of Spain (see Chapter 8, Missions & Adobes). When the Mission was secularized in 1834, grants were given to citizens who applied for property. The State purchased the land around the Old Plaza in 1934, and restored many of its surrounding buildings. The mission was restored by the Catholic church.

Park your car on any city street (no parking meters!) and spend a day wandering. You can begin at the San Juan Bautista State Historic

Park, on the plaza across from the mission, at Second Street between Washington and Mariposa. You'll find the Plaza a lively spot filled with strollers, picnickers and history buffs enjoying the sights and sounds of the town. Your entrance fee entitles you to visit the Plaza Hotel (1858), the Castro House (1840), and the Zanetta House (1868) and its gardens, orchard and livery stable (1874).

Once operated in conjunction with the Hotel, The Livery Stable contains an intriguing collection of horse-drawn equipment. An informative slide presentation on the history of San Juan Bautista, shown at the Plaza Hotel, is included in the tour.

San Juan Bautista's gem is Mission San Juan Bautista, founded on July 24, 1797, and still used as a Catholic Church. The Mission's style differs from its sister missions in that it has three aisles rather than one or two. Once recognized for the nine bells that showed its importance in the mission hierarchy, now only three mission bells survive.

The flat streets and scattering of historic buildings makes San Juan perfect for strolling. At the corner of 2nd and Mariposa, in a small park known as the Spanish Garden, an inviting path will lead you to a rustic log building called the Settler's Cabin. Take a peek inside to see what a simple existence early San Juan settlers had. As you wander, you'll pass other historic buildings (most of which are now private residences), shops, and a wide selection of restaurants.

Try the Donkey Deli at the corner of 3rd and Polk for a refreshing break. This is a different concept in dining: you pay by the ounce. The proprietors are of German ancestry and one of the daily specials is usually German, such as homemade sauerkraut and sausages.

The San Juan Chamber of Commerce puts on a series of special programs throughout the year. The first Saturday of the month is "living history" day, sponsored by the State Historic Park Volunteer Association. Other events include monthly Native American Cultural Workshops; Candlelight Tour and Posada in December; astronomy programs, and an annual All-Indian Market, the first weekend in September.

✳ A visit to San Juan Bautista fits in well with a visit to Pinnacles National Monument, to the south, or as part of the tour described earlier in this chapter, San Jose/Salinas/Santa Cruz.

✳ Santa Cruz

If fun is your main reason for exploring, you've come to the right place. Although the legendary Boardwalk is the main attraction, there's lots more to Santa Cruz than just rides. But that's a good place to start.

Fred Swanton never knew the magnitude of his decision to develop a strip of beachfront property. His legacy would extend far beyond the

Beach Boardwalk Casino, eventually encompassing a full boardwalk with over 50 attractions, games and rides, including two National Historic Landmarks: the 1911 Loof carousel, and the 1924 Giant Dipper.

The latest additions to the Boardwalk include the Astro Canyon Virtual Coaster, Octopus' Garden gift store, Sector 7 Laser Tag Arena, Galaxian 3 Theater 6™, Daytona USA Special and Virtual Reality. If that's not enough, 20 major rides and seven children's rides will keep the whole family happy. And surprisingly, you'll probably find, as we did, that Boardwalk munchies aren't as expensive as you'd expect.

(SANTA CRUZ BEACH BOARDWALK/SEASIDE COMPANY)

The Santa Cruz Boardwalk — some places have all the fun!

Water is, of course, the other main draw. People say Santa Cruz has some of the warmest water on the California coast. On West Cliff Drive, at the west end of the city where it meets the ocean, you can visit the Santa Cruz Surfing Museum, which displays over 50 years of surfing memorabilia.

While you wander around Santa Cruz, you might want to stop at these downtown sites (if you can drag them away from the Boardwalk!): Octagon Museum; Santa Cruz City Museum; Art Museum of Santa Cruz County — workshops for children, and special events. And if your family enjoys a mystery, you'll laugh yourselves silly at the Mystery Spot, 1953 Branciforte Dr., 423-8897. Not far from downtown, this is the place where balls roll uphill, where uphill appears to be downhill, and gravity is defied. We defy you to explain it!

Other things to check out:

Natural Bridges State Beach, home to the largest Monarch butterfly collection in the US (see Chapter 6, Festivals: Monarch Butterfly Migration Festival); Long Marine Laboratory and Aquarium, a marine research and instructional facility of UC Santa Cruz, which includes touch tanks, a dolphinarium and a chance to watch research in progress (see Chapter 2, Animals); the Santa Cruz Municipal Wharf, a prime fishing location where sea lions, pelicans and other sea birds will keep you company.

✳ Santa Cruz to Half Moon Bay (Coast Drive)

Between Santa Cruz and Half Moon Bay, the coastline often competes with neighboring Monterey's for dramatic seascapes. You can marvel at a shoreline carved by the ocean's fury as you enjoy the outstanding views, nature watching, beachcombing and visits to several State parks that make this drive along the Cabrillo Highway (Hwy 1) unforgettable.

From Santa Cruz take Hwy 1 north toward Davenport. Along the way you have the chance to visit both Wilder Ranch State Park and Big Basin Redwoods State Park (see Ch. 3). Big Basin, nine miles southwest of Boulder Creek, was created in 1902 as the first of California's state redwood parks. A drive or walk through the park will take you through dense redwoods and lush foliage with a chance to stop along the way at a small natural history museum. Walk-in and drive-in campsites, 338-6132; handicapped facilities. Wilder Ranch State Park, two miles north of Santa Cruz offers dramatic ocean views from its bluffs. You can tour the restored ranch house grounds and blacksmith shop each weekend from 10-4.

At Davenport you can relax with a snack or a light meal at the Davenport Cash Store, a low-key restaurant/gift shop/inn on the right, going north, not far from Big Basin. And the kids won't want to miss the Davenport Jail Museum, next to the store (open weekends 10-2). While nearby, pull into the Odwalla Juice Company's parking lot and walk up the hill to watch for whales, in season (see Ch. 3, Panorama Points). (Odwalla is no longer open for tours.)

Two miles north of Davenport, look for Swanton Rd. as it heads east from the highway. Named for Fred Swanton, who developed the Santa Cruz Beach Boardwalk, the road winds through canyons and redwoods, eventually coming to the town of Swanton, kept alive by the artisans who own its few homes. After you pass the Seaside Schoolhouse, the road leaves the canyon and at its highest point affords outstanding ocean views as it winds down to its intersection with Hwy 1. This is just one of several scenic redwood drives in the vicinity.

Once back on Hwy 1, as you continue north as you will come to Año Nuevo State Reserve, home of the northern elephant seal. During breeding season (December-March) advance reservations are a necessity. During the rest of the year you can take a less harried stroll, with a naturalist or on your own. The reserve is home to not only the seals but sea lions and birds as well (see Ch. 2, Pets, Animals & Wildlife), and a series of unusual Native American middens (shell mounds); (415) 879-0227.

As you continue north on Hwy 1, the white beacon of Pigeon Point Lighthouse will soon stand out in the distance. The lighthouse sits on a headland six miles south of the Pescadero turnoff. Perched atop rocky outcroppings, this lighthouse is one of the tallest in the United States. For an unusual place to take a vacation, you can rent the former Coast Guard family residences beside the lighthouse through the American Youth Hostel program (298-0670). The lighthouse is open for public tours on Sundays; (415) 879-0633 (see Ch. 3, Panorama Points).

The many beaches nestled into the irregular coastline beneath the lip of the highway offer spots to get out, stretch, picnic or burn off some energy in the tangy, salt air. Pull out to watch kite-flyers, surfers, and sea birds. Some luck and patience might put you in the path of a flock of gawky pelicans, as ours did.

When you reach Pescadero State Beach (see Ch.3, State Beaches), take the bucolic drive along Pescadero Rd., several miles inland to the town of Pescadero, now a glimmer of what it was. At its zenith, it held two saloons, two hotels and many New England-style homes. There are still reminders of the past in Williamson's Country Store, and the Gingerbread Barn. Artichokes, a local crop, are a specialty at Duarte's Tavern and the Beach House at Gazos Creek.

Continue along Pescadero Road, which turns west and becomes Hwy 84, and you'll wind back toward the ocean, through San Gregorio. The Spaniards once considered this spot as a mission site (but decided against it), and in its heyday, San Gregorio was a stagecoach destination for city-folk looking to "get away from it all" at a country resort. The town sits in a valley dappled with eucalyptus and oak, a sleepy little town whose main attraction is the San Gregorio General Store, where you can buy anything from a local history book to a rain slicker.

Regular patrons come to sit at the oak bar worn smooth by many lifted elbows. Once you've passed the town, it's a short hop to Hwy 1, where you can wend your way to Half Moon Bay (see description, this chapter). From here, it's a short hop inland to San Mateo, where you can get Freeway 101 back to San Jose.

☀ Santa Cruz to San Mateo (Inland Route)

An alternate to the oceanside drive north, from Santa Cruz to San Mateo, is the inland route through the redwoods that begins on Hwy 9. Along the way you will have opportunities to stop at several State Parks.

If you haven't already done so, you can stop in Felton, just north of Santa Cruz, to walk across its famous covered bridge (see Ch. 2, Off the Beaten Path, Felton). A sign on the highway directs you there. You're also not far from Roaring Camp and Big Trees Narrow Gauge Railroad (see Ch. 2, Transportation). This could be your best opportunity to take a train ride through the redwoods, but be sure to allow enough time; Roaring Camp can be a whole-day excursion.

As you drive the two-lane highway between Felton and Boulder Creek, (about six miles), you'll soon be surrounded by the cool, towering redwood forests of Henry Cowell State Park (see Ch. 3, Parks). On a warm summer day, the shady redwoods provide not only scenic beauty but a relief from the heat. They also provide the medium for artisans who sell carved goods, from whirligigs to monstrous totems, along the road before you reach Boulder Creek.

Boulder Creek, although quite small, is one of the biggest communities along Hwy 9. If you arrive on a weekend, the Historical Society Museum is open from 2-4. It's at the south end of town in a small commercial center, on the right side of the highway. And if you're curious to see what this one-time lumber town looked like (or if your gang loves pizza), stop at the pizza parlor on your right. Its interior walls are an art gallery of sorts, showcasing historic photos of the town, some many times enlarged.

At this point in your tour, you might want to drive two blocks north and turn left on West Park Av. to 13390, the Boulder Creek Library, 338-7278. The cozy building has a spacious children's area, and a grassy knoll behind the building is just the place to run around and burn off that excess energy before getting back in the car.

As you wind north, following the San Lorenzo River, you'll begin a gradual climb. Just before you reach Hwy 35 (Skyline Drive), you'll have an opportunity to pull off the road into a day use area where you can park the car and look south over Sanborn Skyline County Park and parts of Castle Rock State Park (see Ch. 3, "Panoramas").

If you turn east at Skylonda, on Hwy 84, you'll arrive in the village of Woodside, a community where horses are an important part of daily life. Woodside was once a lumber town, and claimed the county's first sawmill. Today, notable buildings that remain include Woodside Town Hall and The Woodside Store, now a history museum. You'll see Woodside Town Hall, built in 1884, to your left of the intersection of Hwy 84 (Woodside Rd.) and Canada Rd. The Woodside Store (Tripp & Woodside Rds.), was opened in 1854 by Mathias Parkhurst and Dr. Robert Orville Tripp, a dentist. Initially the store served as a library, bank, post office, and dental office. Today, the fastidiously restored, shingled store contains examples of goods typical of the 1880s, like oxen harnesses, and serves as a history museum (see Ch. 2, Museums).

For the last leg of your adventure, follow Canada Rd. past Upper Crystal Springs Reservoir to Hwy. 92 where you will turn east for the brief drive to San Mateo. If time permits, stop at the College of San Mateo's Historical Museum (See Ch. 2, Museums), for an overview of the history of San Mateo County, from the days of the Ohlone Indians through the turn of the century.

8
Missions and Adobes

California Missions: an Introduction

How important were the missions to California? Open up a map. Those words may look like city names, but before there was a city there, the name was already in place, from Basilica San Diego de Alcalá in the south all the way up past San Francisco de Asis — and a few more along the way: Santa Barbara, San Luis Obispo. Is there a big city missing? Not really. Before it became the City of the Angels, Los Angeles belonged to an archangel, San Gabriel, and the mission named for him sat at the crossroads of the west coast of America.

And halfway up the coast, near the bays of San Francisco and Monterey, there are missions in the mountains and along the rivers: San José, in the hills where it could look across the bay, and Santa Clara, a mission that became a university. There's Santa Cruz, overlooking the ocean, and San Juan Bautista in the rich fields inland from the coast; San Antonio de Padua, majestic in a valley of oaks, and Soledad, so lonely that the priests assigned to it begged for relief from the desolation. And on the coast, just where the land turns from sand to rock and the cliffs start rising wildly, sits the tower of Carmel, the mission at the head of them all. Every one of these missions is completely different from the others, in architecture, in history, and especially in the landscape it fills. But they all have something in common. They gave more than their names to the places where they stood; they shaped the California we see today. And one other thing: they're all within a short drive of the city of San José, along the King's Highway.

Catching up with your Fourth-grader: A Quick Mission History

Almost every 4th-grader in California does a "Mission Project" of some kind — it's in the education plan for the whole state. The project may be in the form of a report on a certain mission, or on several of them, a model of a mission, a photo essay, or some other hands-on work. For parents of 4th-graders, that can mean at least three things: find some resources, learn the language the kids are using, and visit a mission. The area around San José offers plenty of first-rate missions to choose from, and information about visiting them is covered in the other pages in this section. And at the end of this section there is a list of useful books and other resources. But first, here's a quick overview of the history of the missions — and some of the terms your 4th-grader may be tossing around.

There are three major phases in the heritage of every mission — the founding (between 1769-1823), secularization (1833-1836), and restoration (from 1893 to the present). Let's match these dates with some background information about the Spanish Empire in America.

✳ Background

When the Spanish Conquistadores arrived in America early in the sixteenth century, their first concerns were with the native empires they conquered. The Aztecs fell in 1521, and the Europeans called the territory New Spain (now Mexico). In 1533, the Incas of South America were defeated, and Spain occupied Peru. There were expeditions into other parts of North America, especially by soldiers looking for gold, but, except for a few ships exploring the coast, California was virtually unknown and unwanted.

By the 17th century, Baja California had been populated with missions, and others were pushed into Texas and New Mexico. Farther west, Padre Kino built missions in what is now Arizona and Sonora, but still there was little interest in the area we call the state of California. Then in the 18th century, in the twilight of the Spanish occupation, a rival appeared — the fur business of Russia was extending itself down the American coast, and suddenly the monarchs of Spain felt they needed to protect their interests.

Padre Junípero Serra and Captain Gaspar de Portolá were sent in 1769 from Baja to what was called Alta (Upper) California or New California to found a series of missions that would bar Russia, or any other country, from claiming the lands Spain felt belonged to her. The plan was to build the missions on the two best bays they knew — San Diego and Monterey. (No one discovered San Francisco Bay until Portolá wandered past Monterey and stumbled on the great bay to the north.) Then, other missions were to stretch along the way between those two points.

The Spanish tried to supply the missions on land routes from Santa Fe, but they failed in the desert. For a brief time a route from the outposts of Arizona and Sonora provided cattle, but then it was blocked by the Yuma Indians. Ultimately the California missions had to be self-sufficient, and they had to be near the sea for contact with the ships. They would be the last and longest reach of Spain into America.

✴ The founding and flourishing of the missions (1769-1823)

One of the facts any 4th-grader can tell you about a mission is its number in the order of founding. That's more than just trivia. In fact, the order reveals some interesting points about California just before 1800.

There were 21 missions in all, and for the record, San Diego can claim its place as the first mission founded (1769). But the region near San José saw the next two go up: San Carlos Borromeo at Carmel (2nd, 1770) and San Antonio de Padua (3rd, 1771). Later came Santa Clara (8th, 1777); then Santa Cruz and Soledad appeared in 1791 (12th and 13th), followed by San José (14th) and San Juan Bautista (15th), both in 1797.

Padre Serra founded the first nine missions and administered them from Carmel until his death in 1784. After the brief tenure of Padre Palóu, Padre Fernín Francisco Lasuén took over as Father-President, founding another nine missions during his 18-year rule. Lasuén also used Carmel as his headquarters until his death in 1803. The missions were at their peaks for just a few decades, but during that time they raised thousands of head of cattle, converted thousands of natives to Christianity, and built dozens of communities along the King's Highway. They were literally outposts of the Spanish Empire in America.

During the period when they flourished, the missions were much more than just churches. They were self-sufficient communities, sometimes protected by nearby military outposts (presidios), but often on their own. Each of them was usually run by just two or three Padres or Fathers — the religious authorities who acted as overseers. The work was done by those Indians the padres had converted — called neophytes, recent converts to the religion — or Mission Indians. These natives lived in a regulated lifestyle where they received shelter and food at the mission, and they practiced the Christian religion.

✴ Secularization (1833-1836)

Political developments changed the course of mission history. After being run by Spanish Franciscan monks for several decades, the missions were shut down by a couple of key events. First, Mexico's independence from Spain in 1821 sent a ripple up to California when the new

Mexican government removed the Spanish priests from power. Then, in 1833, the decree of secularization was issued by the Mexican government, and that forced the missions to return all land except the church itself to the natives from whom it had been taken. As a result, the churches had no source of crops or cattle, and no supply ships from Mexico came north. When Mexico turned the religious possessions over to secular powers, the missions were effectively destroyed.

The plan to secularize the missions had been intended all along. In fact, it was the method used to colonize most of the Spanish-American world, using presidios, missions, and pueblos. Spain would establish a base by the military (a presidio), convert the natives to the Christian religion and Hispanic culture by the authorities (the padres in the missions), then set them free in the secular world of towns (pueblos), usually after about ten years.

But in other areas of New Spain, the population was denser and the natives became like the Europeans more quickly. In California, the mission Indians were never able to work independently in the Hispanic world. The lands which were supposed to be returned to the native populations were bought and sold by other Mexicans, and the Indians got little or nothing. The churches also got nothing and fell into ruin. But just a few years later, the United States pushed into California and took over political control in 1848 through the treaty of Guadalupe-Hidalgo. The U.S. gave the mission buildings back to the Catholic Church, but the church could do very little with unprotected, impoverished, and disintegrating buildings.

✸ Restoration (1893-present)

In the last part of the 19th century, a movement began to rebuild and restore some of the missions. But the term "restoration" can be misleading. While it means reconstructing the churches themselves, each mission is different. Most missions were almost completely destroyed by earthquakes, fires, and simple neglect and erosion. In some cases, later churches replaced the originals.

At San Jose, a wooden church was built in 1868, after an earthquake obliterated the building that had been standing. That wooden church was moved across the bay in 1982 in order to reconstruct a model of an earlier mission. The church at Santa Clara is almost entirely new — it was built in 1928, after a fire burned its predecessor, but it was built as close as possible to the design of the church of 1822. And other missions, including Santa Cruz, have been rebuilt on a smaller scale than the original and serve mainly as chapels today.

The question is, which version of the mission to restore? Most of the restorations are based on the second or third church built on a site. Padre Serra is credited with founding the first nine missions in the chain, but the only building still standing where we know for certain that he celebrated mass is at San Juan Capistrano. Most of the other churches chosen as models for restoration were built after he died. Often the first site showed itself liable to damage. Several missions were lost to floods early in their existence, forcing the next churches to higher grounds. Others were destroyed by earthquakes, and new sites were chosen. At San Juan Bautista, the earthquakes in the early 19th century changed the design several times, as the architects worked on a plan featuring three aisles, then re-thought the large open area and bricked in the arches of the side aisles to make the building stronger. The models for the restored missions are generally dated from the last decade of the 18th century through the first three decades of the 19th.

Missions on San Francisco Bay

One of the most obvious facts about the California missions is that while they share a common history, each is distinct from the others — it has a different shape, a different role in the mission system, and a different fate. The missions of Santa Clara and San José demonstrate this as well as any two can.

Neither of the missions was founded during the first flurry of building, and for a very good reason: at first the Spanish had no idea where San Francisco Bay was located. But when they found out, and when they realized how big and how important it was, they immediately planted missions and presidios there to protect it. In the 16th and 17th centuries, the ships exploring the west coast of America had sailed right by the bay — some going all the way up to what is now Canada and beyond — and never guessed it was there. The narrow Golden Gate could easily be fogged over and the passage into it would be missed. The English sailor Francis Drake (make that English *pirate*, from the Spanish point of view) landed near Point Reyes in the 16th century, but he missed San Francisco Bay too.

The areas the Spanish chose for the first missions had been San Diego, because of its sheltered harbor, and Monterey, because of the glowing description of an early explorer. So in 1769, Gaspar de Portolá came north in search of the bay praised so highly by Sebastián Vizcáino in 1603. But Monterey Bay didn't offer the protection from winds described by Vizcáino, and Portolá went right by it, thinking it couldn't be the right place.

When he got to Half Moon Bay, Portolá knew he had gone too far, but his men reported a large body of water on the other side of the mountains. It was San Francisco Bay. Still, no one had located the inlet to it. That didn't happen until 1775, but when it did, the Spanish government recognized the possibilities of the area and built four types of communities: a presidio to protect the entrance to the bay — San Francisco Presidio, founded in 1776; a pueblo to establish a population in the area — the first town in California, San José, in 1777; and two missions — San Francisco de Asis to the north in October, 1776, and Santa Clara de Asis in the south, just a few months later in January, 1777. Mission San José was built twelve years later, in 1797.

Throughout their history, the three missions on San Francisco Bay served the aims of the padres well. The fathers at Santa Clara baptized 8,536 natives before the end of 1832, according to mission records, the most of any mission in the chain. And combining the three — Santa Clara's 8,536, San José's 6,673, and San Francisco's 6,898 — the missions accounted for more than a fourth of all baptisms at the twenty-one missions in California.

But the appeal of the Santa Clara and San José missions today is less in the statistics of conversions, and more in the heritage of the past that these missions have preserved in very different ways.

✸ Mission Santa Clara de Asis

Santa Clara University, 500 El Camino Real — Box 3217, Santa Clara, CA 95053-3217 ✸ *554-4023*

When you approach Mission Santa Clara, up a palm-lined drive, you might feel as if you're approaching something refined and elegant, rather than a rustic shelter of the past. And when you stroll through the sunlit gardens, with roses rich in geometric patterns, and bright petals of pansies on the ground, and stately buildings around the enclave, you are encountering the great tradition itself. The relief carvings and statues on the face of the mission are a polished finish, the rich veneer of civilization.

The traditions at Santa Clara lie deep, but the rough origins are buried here, like the original cross of 1777, standing now in front of the church, across the street, encased in a redwood reliquary to protect it from the elements. The origins are enclosed, like the old adobe wall, a few hundred feet from the chapel, under a tile roof so the rains can't reach to erode it. These, and a few statues and relics inside the church, are about all that remains of the original mission, delicate reminders of the past, enshrined for their own protection under the modern surface.

There are no pastoral flocks here, no rolling hills fading to the horizon where an ancient padre could confront his calling. The mission is in the heart of a city, the urban center of Santa Clara and San José. But even in the beginning that was the case. The pueblo of San José and the mission of Santa Clara de Asis were built at the same time, and troubles between the secular and the sacred outposts appeared immedi-

ately — the same kinds of troubles that would plague and destroy the mission at Santa Cruz. At Santa Clara, one of the solutions was to bring the two communities closer, and a broad avenue — the Alameda — was created, four miles long under a canopy of trees, joining the mission and the pueblo. It was an urbane solution, an elegant manner of containing human nature.

(SAN JOSE CONVENTION AND VISITORS BUREAU)

Mission Santa Clara de Asis was built by the Spanish government in 1777, the same year they established the first town in California, el Pueblo de San José de Guadalupe (now called San Jose).

But physical nature was not so easily enveloped. Santa Clara suffered from floods early on, heavy rains in 1839, and earthquakes, both in the 19th century and again in the 20th, in 1909 and 1913. But the final blow seemed to come in 1926 when fire destroyed the mission chapel — a fire caused when one of those civilized adjustments to life wore through, the insulated sheaths wrapping electrical wires. The church was a complete loss, and even the heavy iron bells were damaged. But the catastrophe was resolved, and tradition endured. The bells were hung from a make-shift support, and they have continued to ring without a break since 1799. When the church was rebuilt, the designs of 1822 were adopted on the facade, but instead of being painted on, as they had been before, they were carved into statues and stone pilasters.

Inside, the few remaining relics were built into the design as well, and where that was impossible, copies were made. The paintings on the ceiling had been created by the Mexican artist Agustín Dávila in a sophisticated style where angels peer through clouds that seem to surround a hole in the ceiling that leads up the heavens — a technique borrowed from the grand tradition of Europe rather than from the home-spun habits of America. After the fire of 1926, the patterns of the original paintings were copied onto the ceiling again. The interior seems different from those in the other missions. There's more of the rational feel of the Enlightenment instead of the piety of rustic chapels. The aura is sophisticated and refined.

Sometimes children seem to act differently at Santa Clara. The mission offers more than a sense of a dim past, an echo of what used to be. The gardens are bright, the buildings are polished, and the world seems to be more elevated than it does outside these walls of tradition. It's a place to experience what a real university feels like — not just a catalog of courses, but the heritage of a culture.

At Santa Clara, the remains of the mission are encased in modern shelters, and the legacies of our culture are sheathed in the idea of a university. It is an elegant way to recall our past.

✹ Mission San José

P.O. Box 3159 Fremont, CA 94539 (43300 Mission Blvd., Fremont)
✹ (510) 657-1797

Mission San José is a house of contradictions. It's haunted by antiquity, yet it's the newest structure to be built. The exterior is plain, almost nondescript, but the decorations inside glow like jewels. Sometimes it enticed the neophytes with ethereal chants and hymns, and sometimes it served as a base to hunt down hostile natives. And while most missions gave their names to the cities that followed them, San José took its title from the pueblo nearby.

The town of San José began in 1777 — the first town established in New California — by orders of the Spanish government to protect San Francisco Bay, along with the Presidio of San Francisco and the Missions of San Francisco and Santa Clara. But it was not until 1797 that Mission San José itself was founded. Once the original missions had been established, the mission chain grew by filling in gaps between the missions to allow for easier travel on *El Camino Real*. Again San José went against the norm, since it didn't bring any missions closer together — it's on a short spur to the northeast of Santa Clara, while the King's Highway heads northwest from Santa Clara up the peninsula to San Francisco. But it sits where it has a vantage of the entire bay. When the weather was right, San José could see both Santa Clara and San Francisco.

Ironically, the mission is not in San José at all, but in Fremont. And even in an urban corner of the modern world, Mission San José stands before a hillside, rugged and strong rather than urbane and sophisticated. Its imposing shape today is the same as it was in 1840.

But it wasn't always that way. San José suffered through natural disasters, as did the other missions, and after secularization, it served the California gold rush as a trading store. When an earthquake leveled the adobe church in 1868, the new structure was a peaked wooden church, like those of New England. That building stood for over a century, until it was moved across the bay to Burlingame in 1985 to allow a church to be built whose design came from the mission period. Materials and designs were modeled on the original plans, so the new structure looks as if it is, in fact, old. One of the exceptions to making an exact copy is in the adobe blocks. Old adobe buildings had a problem when the tile roofs were removed — the walls eroded in the rain. The new adobe used in the San José mission contains asphalt to prevent its destruction by the elements.

Part of the past that Mission San José evokes comes from the cemetery, a patch of toppling monuments and marble slabs on the north side of the church. You enter it from the sanctuary itself, and the sense of walking between death and consolation is made stronger by the carved skull and crossbones above the door — a motif denoting cemeteries that is common throughout the California missions.

The carvings and statues inside on the altar and along the side walls catch the light from high windows and throw out a brilliant gold and green in the midst of the shadows — hammered copper, polychrome wood, and silver-painted candlesticks. Centuries ago the thick walls and simple wooden ceiling must have echoed with the sounds of hymns and concerts. In the 1820s Father Durán imported instruments from Mexico, and made his own when he couldn't find others, and taught the mission Indians to play. But not all of the native peoples enjoyed the harmonies of the Christian world. Mission San José was one of the bases where military expeditions set out to punish warring and rebellious tribes. These sounds too echo from the ceiling and haunt the high walls of the church.

Outside the church, near a garden of herbs and a fountain, lie long wooden beams from the century before. Once these lost rooms by the church were covered, and the beams were the supports of the roof that fell.

And to put the prosaic beside the moonlit, the reason by the mist, there is a museum and a gift shop, with statues, tools, and the furniture of the original church. There's even a slide show, with the presentation times available in the gift shop. Yet that seems right too — a flickering evocation of light in the surrounding darkness.

In one sense, Mission San José is the newest of the missions available to the public, since it was the one mission of the chain not to have been restored or replicated until the last few years. And it echoes the hymns of a dimmer age, when candles glowed in a human darkness. Now it looms on the hillside as it once did, above the cemetery, above the bay, brooding upon the modern world that passes by.

Missions South of San Jose

The missions within reach of San Jose on easy excursions have completely different characters and separate histories, but they are also a part of the larger story that weaves all 21 of the California missions into whole cloth. It's the story of the time when Spain moved north to a land it thought was empty. It's the time when the natives of California encountered both good and bad Europeans, sometimes having their lives enriched, and most of the time losing their land and heritage. And it's the time when the rest of the world discovered California, and fought for control of it. It's the story of how the Indians, Spain, England, Russia, Mexico, and finally the United States defined the cultures of the future.

Among the missions within a few hours drive south of San Jose are five churches, starting with Mission Santa Cruz, a model one-third the size of the original, high on a hill above the San Lorenzo River, over-looking Monterey Bay and the Pacific Ocean. Another hour south is Mission Nuestra Señora de la Soledad, a lonely outpost two hundred years ago, and a church isolated even today. And spaced like three points on a five-armed star are three of the finest of the mission chain, all built in different styles, but all among the best preserved and restored of the California missions: San Juan Bautista to the southeast, San Antonio de Padua to the south, and San Carlos Borromeo de Carmelo on the coast in Carmel, between Big Sur and Monterey.

A tour of all five of these missions on the same day would be far too time-consuming to allow more than a wave at the missions as you passed by, but combinations can be put together to suit any taste. Santa Cruz is the closest to San Jose and could be combined with any of the others, especially San Carlos Borromeo down the coast or San Juan Bautista inland from Monterey Bay. Soledad and San Antonio are also a natural pairing since they are the two farthest south, but Soledad is also a good match for either San Juan Bautista or Carmel. And San Antonio has good connecting roads to San Carlos Borromeo, either down the Carmel Valley highway or on a spectacular hour's drive through the Santa Lucia Range to Big Sur and north to Carmel. Choose the missions that suit your fancy, and enjoy the trip. Even the farthest of these missions is less than two hours away, and besides, you'll be riding on the King's Highway.

🟊 Mission Santa Cruz

126 High St., Santa Cruz, CA 95060. From San Jose take route 17 south and exit at River Street. 🟊 *426-5686*

It's only a skip over the hill from San Jose to Santa Cruz, a 45-minute drive on route 17 through a mountain of redwood trees to the northern end of Monterey Bay, and the city of Santa Cruz.

Here is the mission that might have been. It seemed to have everything — a spot on a hill overlooking the bay, good land and climate, and other missions nearby — especially San Carlos Borromeo, headquarters for all the missions, just across the water in Carmel. It seemed to the padres that all it needed was a bell ringing the hours. But as they say in real estate, location is everything, and for Santa Cruz that meant the town of Branciforte right next door. The church was here first, and Spanish law said no town could be built close to a mission, but in came the vagabonds, and the troubles began. Instead of being the best mission on the bay, it was the scene of the first autopsy in California history. Seems a few neophytes did in a padre, and got away with it for a couple of years, but murder will out, and when it did the Governor ordered seven conspirators flogged.

Then in 1818 the pirate Hyppolite de Bouchard came by, and there went the neighborhood. The residents of the mission fled, the smugglers of Branciforte raided the goods that were left, and that was that. Bouchard didn't even have to land. Later some of the buildings collapsed, an earthquake in 1857 knocked down the rest of the church, and a flood caused by the quake roared up the river. It was time.

The adobe church was left in ruins, replaced by a wooden one until 1931, when a replica one-third the size of the original was built. And even then, so many of the records of the church had been lost, the builders didn't know which side to put the bell tower on. They had to rely on a painting done after the collapse, by a painter who based it on the descriptions of local residents. That's what's standing today, along with the Mission Santa Cruz Adobe, remnants of a barracks from the early 19th century.

Today, the towering Church of the Holy Cross stands across from the replica of the mission, and pleasant parks are all around the mission's area. The mission chapel is still used, and a museum and gift shop are attached. The appeals of the Santa Cruz mission include the beautiful area it is in and the parks near to the mission. In many ways the place today is better than the star-crossed mission of two centuries ago.

The population at Santa Cruz was always the smallest of the missions. During what should have been its prime, the mission never overcame the abuse from Branciforte or recovered from the natural disasters that knocked down the walls. But now, 200 years later, the mission finally matches the setting — today there are ocean breezes, the sound of a bell on a cool morning, and a chapel on a hill above Monterey Bay.

✸ Mission San Juan Bautista

P.O. Box 400, San Juan Bautista, CA 95045 (2nd and Mariposa Streets, San Juan Bautista). From Highway 101, exit on Highway 156 east (towards Hollister). San Juan Bautista is three miles east, and the mission is one block east of 156. ✸ *623-4528*

The fault line runs right through here. And so does El Camino Real. If you stand on a wooden platform just outside the mission church of San Juan Bautista, you can trace the twin trails of San Andreas and the padres out across the fields of mustard flowers, one threatening to rupture the earth, the other promising to rend the firmament. The first thin line shows the resistance when one part of the earth slides by another, and the second marks the friction where the past rubs against the future. This is the place where the San Andreas fault runs north to the bay, and where the Franciscan fathers of two hundred years ago followed the shattered route of earthquakes in building the King's Highway.

The threat to open the earth is real — and it's happened a number of times. In 1800, the ground shook for six days in a row, and some reports tell of the padres sleeping outside. And in 1906, when the big quake leveled San Francisco, San Juan Bautista was just south of the point where the earth split apart. The mission lost several walls during that shaking. And to make matters more complicated, another of California's major faults, the Hayward Fault, splits from the San Andreas just a few miles down the road, at Hollister. The Hayward Fault is the one responsible for the

The mission bell at San Juan Buatista.

(BRIAN BATES)

Great Quake of 1868, the one that flattened Mission San José. And yet, despite the records of jolts and falling walls, the church itself still stands, something many missions cannot claim. And even more: it's one of the few missions that has functioned without a major interruption for the last two centuries.

Today the mission is on the edge of a state historic park, the oldest building among several with more than a century of status. The mission is not a part of the historic park, however. It still functions as an active church with local parishioners. But the setting makes the past very real. Across the open plaza are the Zanetta House and a stable, two of the younger occupants, at a mere century and a quarter old. The Castro House and Plaza Hotel, dating from 1840 and 1814, respectively, line the south edge of the plaza, while the north side remains open — looking out to the rodeo grounds, the King's Highway, and the fault line itself. But the line that divides the religious church from the secular park is a shared boundary, not a barrier. At times there was friction between the two sides, especially during secularization, but the animosity that destroyed Mission Santa Cruz never broke the community of San Juan Bautista. (The San Juan Bautista State Historic Park is described separately in Chapter 7, Day Trips.)

The arches that line the plaza and house the monastery recall the days of Spanish California — cool shadows escaping from the California sun and the echo of sandals down the long dappled walk. Today the mission's museum and gift shop share part of the old monastery, and the museum is one of the best in the mission chain. Rooms have been restored to show the workings of the original — the dining room and library, displays of the rich, braided vestments, and the music the mission was so famous for. A number of stories can be told about how the Indians were won over to the padres through the playing of the organ or the hurdy-gurdy. Some of the instruments and music books are on display. Two of the four walls of the mission quadrangle have fallen, but the gardens are enclosed by the "L" shape of the monastery and church.

The church itself is unlike any other in the mission chain. The interior is the biggest of them all, and it is the only one with three aisles — an innovation which the padres backed away from when earthquakes hit early in the 19th century. They quickly walled up the arches to strengthen the building, leaving a long, narrow center aisle. During the restoration of 1976, the side walls were rebuilt — they had collapsed in the San Francisco earthquake of 1906 — and the arches opened up again. The bell wall, or campanario, was erected at that time as well. Behind the altar six distinctive arches form a striking tableau, with statues framed by arches and backed by rich red hanging cloth. Yet despite its size and the elegant display, the church has a homey feel — look for the tiles where animals left their footprints in the floor. The line between history and current use, showplace and functioning church, is there — but you have to look to see it.

When the earth slides along a fault line it creates a scarp, a steep ridge where one side jumps up as the other passes by, a dividing line that shows where one world ends and another begins. At San Juan Bautista, the scarp is just past the cemetery, and on top of it are seats for the rodeo grounds, bleachers over the fault itself and the old path of the padres. It's easy to cross over lines in the town of San Juan Bautista.

✳ Mission Nuestra Señora de la Soledad

36641 Fort Romie Road, Soledad, CA 93960. Exit Highway 101 on Arroyo Seco Road south of the town of Soledad. ✳ *678-2586*

As you look around, you might wonder, Why build a mission here? The land is flat and windswept, with a ridge of mountains to the west, and in the summer a nearly dry river bed a short distance away. And that's why the mission is here. There was virtually nothing between Mission San Antonio in the mountains to the south and Mission San Carlos Borromeo in Carmel, a distance of about 100 miles. So Mission Nuestra Señora de la Soledad — Our Lady of Solitude — became the stopover on the dusty road.

It never really prospered. Most priests sent to Soledad did all they could to be reassigned somewhere else, and the average tour of duty was no more than a year. Only one priest stayed longer — Father Florencio Ibanez, who endured from 1803 until 1818. Like all missions, Soledad had its share of epidemics of measles and other diseases, but it added the problem of river flow. Rivers in the inland areas of California are virtually dry in the summer, but torrential in the rainy season, and the Salinas and Arroyo Seco are no different. Floods in 1824, 1828, and 1832 damaged the church, and after secularization, the tiles of the roof were sold, and the adobe walls began to wear away.

The mission today is small, but it contains an interesting museum and gift shop. The bell at the corner of the church is the original, sent from Mexico in 1794. Mounted on an imposing beam between the adobe wall and a short tower, it echoes the isolation of the mission itself. One of the most interesting parts of Soledad lies around the outside of the mission yard. It looks at first like some eroded sandstone of the southwest, but then you realize that these were the original walls, scoured now and drooped into brown mounds, the earthy remains of what died in the middle of the 19th century.

But the gardens themselves are lush — grass and herbs and flowers flowing around the drier residents, cactus and succulents that hoard their waters against the dust and wind.

Inside, it's cool, and small, and simple, and somehow in the expanse of empty dust and heat of the Salinas Valley, it feels like a place to stay for more than a few minutes. Soledad is a reminder that California history has as much to do with endurance and work as with lush windfalls and easy beauty. Here, in the promised land, is a stopover in solitude.

(BRIAN BATES)

Remote yet beautiful, the Mission San Antonio de Padua is a jewel of the Spanish age in California, the third mission established along el Camino Real (the King's Highway).

✳ Mission San Antonio de Padua

P.O. Box 803, Jolon, CA 93928. (Mission Creek Road, 6 miles from entrance to Fort Hunter-Liggett) ✳ *385-4478*

What comes to mind when you think of San Antonio de Padua? Fragments of a landscape: Grass first — green in the spring, and tall; then tawny in the sun when the rains stop. Hills and a winding stream, and the road up to a long field. Oaks — California oaks, molded to the hillside, nested in the dips and valleys, dark green against the straw-colored hills. Then the mission: adobe arches across the field, and an olive tree, brought here long ago, and the dark red bricks of the facade, pushed out away from the church like a cut-out front, and the sun low on the arches and the long shadows of the trees in the grass.

This is why you came. Whatever other missions you have seen, this is the vision that recalls them all.

But this is off the highway, and the question comes up, Why wasn't the mission built on El Camino Real? The answer, of course, is obvious: It was. This is the route the padres walked. It's 101 that detours from the King's Highway.

In the first days, when the padres headed north to Monterey from San Diego, they mapped potential sites along the way. They followed the coast at first — in fact, the mission scheduled to be built after San Diego and San Carlos Borromeo was San Buenaventura, where the city of Ventura lies today, along the ocean front; but that mission was delayed. The explorers went west along the shore, then north to an area rampant with bears, a site which later became San Luis Obispo and which saved both San Antonio and Carmel from starvation some years later when hunters remembered the game. The padres went out to the ocean, to Morrow Bay, then up the coast. But north of what is now San Simeon, the mountains fell steeply into the sea, and the route was impassable. A way led inland, and the priests followed this to a stream in a valley filled with oaks. And this was the place Father Serra remembered when he needed a site for a mission south of Carmel, the one he called San Antonio de Padua de los Robles, the third mission in California.

Today, about 20 miles south of Soledad on Highway 101, near King City, County Road G14 (Jolon Road) goes southwest to the town of Jolon and Mission San Antonio de Padua. And from the south, G18, also called Jolon Road, goes northwest from a place near Bradley. Both of these roads wind loosely through the Santa Lucia Mountains to the mission, located on the Hunter-Liggett Military Reservation in the San Antonio River Valley. You will need to stop at the checkpost to enter the Reservation, but there are no problems in getting to the mission. (If you plan to continue to the coast on the Nacimiento Road, you might ask the guard at the checkpoint about the condition of the road, especially in winter or early spring. Usually, the condition is excellent. Also, check to see if any maneuvers are scheduled that might close some of the area; after all, this is a military reservation.)

Because of its isolation from modern cities, Mission San Antonio shows clearly how a mission complex functioned two hundred years ago. Padre Buenaventura Sitjar, who helped found the mission in 1771 and served as its leader until his death in 1808, combined engineering with linguistics and art. The water system he built ran for miles and included dams and reservoirs, holding ponds and millraces. But Sitjar did more than build the aqueducts; he also compiled a 400-page dictionary of the Mutsun language. And in the wing where the museum is today, you can see paintings used for musical instructions to the mission Indians. On one wall, an enormous hand and colored notes on a clef show the teaching methods of the padres. The museum at San Antonio is extensive, filling a number of rooms behind the arches. At the end of the wing, a huge wine vat illustrates another of the industries of San Antonio. But more than vineyards, these hills are horse and cattle country, and leather and branding irons hang on the walls in the courtyard.

The chapel itself is long and narrow. The church at San Juan Bautista is the largest mission chapel, with outside measurements of 188 feet by 72. But San Antonio, only 40 feet wide, runs 200 feet long. From the wooden entry, the church is like the valley and the aisle is a river running to a distant altar. The facade itself stands out from the chapel like a ridge in the mountains, a solid brickwork bellwall connected to the church through a vault.

But the reality of Mission San Antonio is more than the parts of its buildings and the ruins of the waterways. Standing outside the chapel, or in the shadows of the arches, you can look across the valley, through the grasses and the oaks, and see the shadows of the Spanish age. This is why you came. Here you remember all of the missions, the padre's vision of California itself.

(BRIAN BATES)

Kids of any age can have fun exploring California's history, beginning with its Missions.

When you leave Mission San Antonio...

A short distance to the south are the San Antonio and Nacimiento Reservoirs, beautiful recreational and nature preserves, especially good for camping. And there are interesting routes heading back north from San Antonio. One, of course, is to return on Jolon Road to 101, then go north to Salinas and either west on Highway 1 to Monterey and Carmel or north to the other missions and back to San Jose. Another is to take Road G16 west off 101 halfway to Soledad, then drive up the beautiful Carmel Valley Road. And, for the more adventurous, there's the Nacimiento Road across the mountains to Highway 1 at the town of Lucia, just south of Big Sur. Some guidebooks have hesitated to recommend this road, but we have found it to be in good condition, two relatively wide lanes with grades and curves, but not a difficult road to drive. At 25 to 30 mph, it is just under an hour to the coast, and the scenery is spectacular. The road rises from 1,000 to 4,000 feet, then drops to sea level at the coast. It is as easy a road to drive as some stretches of Highway 1. The Carmel Mission is another half hour up the coast.

✷ San Carlos Borromeo de Carmelo

3080 Rio Road, Carmel, CA 93923. ✷ *624-3600*

The Carmel Mission may be the gemstone in the chain of California missions. It was the headquarters of the system, and Father Serra spent the last years of his life here, consecrating it in death as well as in life. The power of ecclesiastical California emanated from Carmel throughout the mission era, and after secularization and decay, San Carlos Borromeo regained its stature in its 20th century restoration. The rebuilding of the church, under the direction of Harry Downie, took almost fifty years, beginning in the 1930s; but when it was done it was one of the most complete of any mission, along with San Juan Bautista, San Antonio de Padua, and La Purísima Concepción. The fountains splash in the gardens, the ruby bougainvillea cascades over the walls, the bell tolls its deep voice, and the sun fills the plaza.

But step inside Father Serra's room. There's a plank bed, a chair, a wooden writing table. The worldly comforts of the padre are summed up in rough boards and hard edges. The grandeur that is the Carmel Mission is built on the rugged life of the California frontier. The jewel has the texture of adobe walls and the feel of cold stone fountains. The power of its soul lies in the cemetery beneath the trees.

It was in 1769 that Father Serra and Captain Portolá headed north to begin the last great reach of Spanish Empire into America. They left Baja for San Diego on the first leg of the journey to Monterey Bay. Portolá intended to expand and protect the Spanish world from the Russians to the north, while Serra expected to expand and protect the Christian world against the heathen beliefs of a backward land.

Then, in San Diego, reality set in. The ships that sailed from Mexico were beds of scurvy. Most of the sailors died, and with them the plans for the salvation of California were nearly buried as well. But Portolá went ahead, and Serra founded his mission, and with what the padre thought to be a sign from heaven, the enterprise was saved when relief supplies appeared at the last minute.

But San Diego was just the first stop on the way to the north. Monterey was the place the Spanish wanted, and even if it wasn't the harbor described in wonder centuries before, it was to be the military and religious heart of New California. Perhaps if San Francisco Bay had been discovered earlier, San José would have been the center of this world — even though it was built later, San José was the first town to be founded in California — but in 1769 it was Monterey. After altercations with the military leaders, Father Serra moved his center to the south, and Carmel assumed its mantle of sacred power. The administrative heart of the California missions had begun to beat.

From his headquarters in Carmel, Father Serra founded nine missions in all before his death in 1784. His successor, Padre Lasuén, was as energetic as Serra had been and founded nine more missions by the time he died in 1803. Serra and Lasuén were buried side by side within the stone church of San Carlos Borromeo, which had evolved from a rough wood structure built in 1771.

The mission today shows its strength in the stoneworks, in the bell towers and domes, the columns and the cool thick walls, but the power is shrouded in the beauty of the gardens. You first see the chapel through a vine covered archway, down a walk past a fountain. A window like a scalloped diamond punctuates the doorframe, and inside, a parabolic vault covers the sanctuary. The simple shape frames an elegant altar. In the rooms off the chapel are the monuments — a statue of the Virgin that Serra brought from Baja to San Diego and Monterey, and the sepulchre of Serra himself and Lasuén.

The museum that fills the wing near the church shows the world of the mission, complete within itself: kitchen and dining hall, the padre's study, and the sparse private quarters. And in the few square feet allotted for each, thousands of Indians are interred alongside the church.

But it's in the patio that the mission shows its rich colors. On the other side of the chapel from the cemetery, outside the barren room of Father Serra and the tomb of the founders, is the plaza of the great fountain and the side of the bell tower, the open flow of sunshine and the rich red bougainvillea cascading over the stones. The truth of San Carlos Borromeo de Carmelo lies in the union of its opposites: cemetery and plaza, sumptuous altar and sparse quarters, rough stone and jewel.

And from those contradictions of shadow and sunlight, California was born.

Books and Resources
for Mission Projects

There are a number of books about the missions available, although many of them are simply collections of beautiful photographs — after all, every one of the missions looks good. (Don't forget your camera when you visit, but be sure to check on restrictions on picture-taking, especially with flash — see the tips at the end of this chapter.) In the books with more content, there's one other thing to watch out for. Many of them were published in the 1950s and 1960s, and our attitudes have changed quite a bit since then, especially regarding the treatment of the native peoples by the arriving Europeans. Some of the books have a decidedly patronizing attitude toward the lifestyles of the Indians. And, to extend those insults further, some of the later books just copied information from the earlier ones without revising or reconsidering the data. When you read the books listed below, or any others you may find, please use your judgment about those attitudes.

For several decades, the most popular introduction to all the missions has been **The California Missions,** put out by Sunset Books (Lane Publishing Company: Menlo Park, California, Soft Cover Edition 1979). It's over 300 pages long and has plenty of pictures. Especially interesting are the photos from the past, including some from the 19th century. This book is available at almost all large book stores.

One of the most attractive books is **The Missions of California** by Stanley Young, with photographs by Melba Levick (Chronicle Books: San Francisco, 1988). The emphasis is on the pictorial side. Like the Sunset book, this one is also widely available.

Bellerophon Books of Santa Barbara has produced a series of books published between 1985 and the present. The subjects are more unusual, which makes them very interesting. One is **Saints of the California Missions,** featuring a page of information about each saint and a color photograph of a mission painting showing that saint. Another is **The Decoration of the California Missions,** an extensive description of the interior paintings and designs of the churches. Both of these books are by Norman Neuerburg.

Henry Miller was an artist and traveler who visited the missions in 1856, drawing them and reporting on their condition. Bellerophon has reproduced his works in a book titled **California Missions: The Earliest Series of Views Made in 1856.** And there are two 7.5" × 17" books called **California Missions To Cut Out,** featuring parts of the missions to use scissors and tape on. All of Bellerophon's books are inexpensive (usually under $10). They can be found in educational book stores and teacher supply stores.

Along the King's Highway: The Missions of California is a set of multi-media materials about all of the missions, available for Macintosh computers from Brian Bates Productions in Fair Oaks, California (916/ 962-1052). The program includes photographs, essays on history and architecture, layouts and designs of individual missions, and other information in an interactive format that features each mission on its own and ties all 21 together in California history.

For material on individual missions, especially for use by 4th-graders, Mary Null Boulé has put together 21 booklets, one for each mission. There are three sections in each book. The first is an introduction to Father Serra and the missions overall (the same text in all books), followed by a description of the one mission in particular and a history of that mission. As a 4th-grade teacher, the author has written the books to be used directly by the young scholars, and she includes drawings and a glossary of unfamiliar terms. Each book is 25 pages long. The booklets are sold at the missions. Prices vary by the location of the mission, ranging from about $4 to $8.

Langtry Publications in Chatsworth, California has published several books on specialized subjects: **The Indians and the California Missions, Father Junipero Serra the Traveling Missionary,** and **California Mission Projects & Activities** among them. These are also written for young readers, and the information is extensive. **The Indians and the California Missions,** by Linda Lyngheim, is over 150 pages long.

For background and general reading, Richard Henry Dana's book **Two Years Before the Mast** tells the story of sea trade along the California coast in the 1830s. The autobiographical account of Dana's experience, it was first published in 1840, and has been regarded as a classic ever since. Helen Hunt Jackson's novel **Ramona** is the most famous story of romance set during the mission period.

Here's a special treat: Mark Preston has written **California Mission Cookery: A Vanished Cuisine — Rediscovered** (Border Books: Albuequerque, 1994). The book provides an historical introduction and over 250 recipes, based on the foods and preparations of more than a hundred years ago.

And, of course, every mission has its own materials, some of which are simple pamphlets and handouts, and others extensively researched books. (Sydney Temple's book **The Carmel Mission from Founding to Rebuilding**, Valley Publishers, Fresno, 1980, is an adult-level, detailed history 166 pages long.) Contact the gift shops at each mission to see what's available. Most will send you some materials requested over the phone, but remember that it costs to do this. Some missions charge a small fee, and for those that don't, a few dollars donation would be appropriate.

Tips along the Missions Roads

The missions offer their own kind of enjoyment, and they ask a few small favors from you as well. Here are a few things you might want to do, and a few mistakes to avoid.

☀ Basic Information

While preparing this book, we found that the people working at the missions were, without exception, outstandingly helpful and courteous. When in doubt, please ask these people for advice or for information on what the regulations are. Either call them before you visit (phone numbers are listed by the missions themselves) or ask when you arrive.

☀ Admission

The cost to get in varies at each mission. Some are free, some ask for a small donation, and a few charge a few dollars for admission to a museum. As with all of the other items on this list, the best information comes from calling the mission directly, especially since prices can vary at different times of the year and for different age visitors. The phone numbers are listed under the individual missions. Most missions are open from about 9:00 am to 4:00 pm, but again, call the mission directly for the most up-to-date information. Ask as well about the times for church services so that you can schedule your visit at a time when you can inspect an empty chapel, or when you can participate if you would like to. Remember that the missions may also schedule special events, such as large groups participating in the rite of First Communion. And many of the missions are in demand as the site of a wedding. Check ahead.

✳ Clothes

In our informal world, it is easy to forget that an interesting place to visit may also have other uses. In Mexico, some churches do not allow people to enter if they are dressed in shorts or a halter top. While the California missions are more tolerant of comfort, be respectful of those who use the missions as a place of worship. Casual clothes are certainly acceptable.

✳ Photography

Some of the missions have restrictions on photography, although in general the regulations are minimal. Most of the limitations are on the use of strobes (flashes). The bright light can damage the colors or cloth of some of the items in a museum, so sometimes flash photography is not allowed. Usually signs are posted, but it is a good idea to ask as well. Some missions request no pictures at all be taken in the church areas proper, although the missions near San José have allowed pictures in most areas.

Here's another reason not to use flash: On most small cameras, the built-in flash has a range of about 20 to 30 feet or less. If you try to take a flash picture of something 50 feet away, there will probably not be enough light with or without a strobe. (If the distance is much more than across a large living room, it may be too far for the flash to be effective.) Become familiar with the range of your camera before your visit to avoid disappointment later. One last tip — if the museum allows flash photography and the subject you want to shoot is in a glass case, put your camera as close as possible to the glass to avoid a reflection of the strobe light. (Get as close to the glass as possible to avoid reflections without flash lighting as well.) And, of course, if the church is in use, show respect for the worshipers in how you use the camera.

✳ Food

Most of the missions — Santa Clara, San José, Carmel, Santa Cruz, and San Juan Bautista — are in places where groceries, snacks, or restaurant meals are easy to buy. But Soledad and San Antonio are more isolated. There are some facilities in the towns of Soledad and Jolon, but none right at the mission (except for a possible vending machine).

✳ Weather, Temperature, and Outdoor Factors

All of the missions have the potential to enjoy the heat of a California summer. On the coast, the weather may be cool and breezy even when it is warm elsewhere. Missions farther inland, especially San Antonio, Soledad, and San Juan Bautista, can be very hot in the summer. Remember your sun screen, a hat for shade, and sunglasses to shield the glare from the white adobe walls.

✳ Special Factors

Mission Santa Clara is a part of the University of Santa Clara. Permits for special photography and access to the mission are regulated by the university. Normally there is no difficulty in visiting, but please contact the mission officials for special requests.

Mission San Antonio de Padua is located on a military base (Hunter-Liggett Military Reserve), and you will need to stop at a checkpoint on the way in. At times, some nearby areas might be closed due to special maneuvers. Usually, there is no inconvenience at all, but check at the entry booth or call ahead if you want to be sure. The Nacimiento road from San Antonio to Highway 1 on the coast may be subject to repairs or to military movements. Again, there are usually no problems at all. If you or your children suffer from motion sickness, both the Nacimiento road and Highway 1 might be places to consider motion sickness pills.

Adobes

Between the late 18th and mid-19th centuries, a readily available mixture of clay, straw and water, called adobe, was often used to construct California buildings. These buildings, often personal dwellings, later took on the generic name "adobe."

The San Jose region has a series of adobes, many open to the public, that can give you an understanding and appreciation of the life of that

era. Even if you cannot enter the buildings, a drive past or walk around can elicit respect for the ingenuity and the life of northern California's pioneers.

✳ Juana Briones de Mirada Adobe

Old Trace Rd. east of W. Fremont Av., near junction with Arastradero Rd., Palo Alto (private residence).

What remains of the Briones adobe — the east wall, covered patio and main entrance — stands on land Briones purchased in 1844 as a Mexican land grant. It was then known as Rancho La Purísima Concepción.

✳ Boronda Adobe

Corner Boronda Rd./W. Laurel Dr., Salinas. Open M-F, 10-2; Sun, 1-4. ✳ 757-8085

One of the oldest buildings in the area, this adobe was built between 1844-48 by José Eusebio Boronda and early settler and rancher. It's an example of "Monterey Colonial" architectural style, which combined elements of New England's architecture with the California tradition. Adjacent Lagunita School dates from 1848.

✳ Castro Adobe

San Juan Bautista State Historic Park, San Juan Bautista.

This two-story adobe was built by General Jose Castro following his appointment as prefect of Northern California. Castro sold the adobe and 400 acres of land to the Patrick Breen family, survivors of the Donner Party. The restored adobe contains furnishings from the 1870s.

✳ Charles Brown Adobe

Wunderlich County Park, west of Woodside; c. 1839. Not open to the public. ✳ (415) 851-1210

One-time whitewashed adobe home of Charles Brown who constructed San Mateo County's first sawmill on the bank of Alambique Creek. The sawmill was patterned after John Sutter's mill in Coloma, where gold was discovered in 1848. The adobe was later converted to an ice house by the Folger family (of Folger's coffee), who once owned the property.

✺ Higuera Adobe

47300 Rancho Higuera Rd., Fremont.

At the foot of Mission Peak in the Warm Springs area of Fremont, the Higuera Adobe is the last of seven adobes built in 1840 on Fulgencio Higuera's ranch. It consists of a large main room and two small bedrooms.

✺ Peralta Adobe (see Chapter 1)

✺ Richardson Adobe

One mile south of Soledad on US101.

Built by William Richardson in 1843 on Los Conches Rancho, this adobe served as stage stop, post office and house for tenant farmers. It was restored by the State as part of the Los Coches State Wayside Camp and Los Coches Adobe State Historical Monument.

✺ Roberto-Sunol Adobe

770 Lincoln Av., San Jose.

Built in 1836 by a native Californian, Roberto Belermino, this one-story dwelling was later enlarged by Antonio Sunol (in 1847). Later still, in 1853, the second story and balcony were added by Captain Stefano Splivalo. It's now a commercial building and not open to the public.

✺ Santa Clara Women's Club Adobe

3260 The Alameda. From I-880 take Bascom Exit toward Santa Clara (there are 2 Bascom Exits; be sure to take the Santa Clara one). Turn rt. on Benton to The Alameda. Turn right and park on the street. You'll be within walking distance of the University and South Bay Historical Railroad Society as well. ✺ 296-9830

Built about 1790, this California Historical Landmark, No. 249, is one of the oldest adobes in California. Today, the adobe is used as headquarters for the Santa Clara Women's Club. If you happen along while a club member is on-site you'll be welcomed inside. In any case, step into the courtyard to enjoy the garden. Notice the tiles on the courtyard wall, the deep window ledges and narrow doorways characteristic of adobe architecture.

✸ Santa Cruz Mission State Historic Park

126 High St., Santa Cruz, corner Emmett/High Sts. Free. ✸ 426-5686

History and architecture buffs will enjoy a tour of the adobe house located in Santa Cruz Mission State Historic Park. The adobe was built in 1822 to house Native Americans who worked at the Mission. It is the last remaining structure of Mission Santa Cruz, and the only authentically restored Native American living quarters in the entire California Mission chain.

✸ Vallejo Adobe

Located behind Mission Adobe Garden Center, in Vallejo Adobe Historical Park, Fremont ✸ (510) 791-4340. Accessible only during nursery hours, which vary ✸ (510) 796-7575. You can walk around the outside of the adobe, but it's only open to those who rent it for special events.

The adobe was built in 1843 by Don José Vallejo, acting chief administrator for Mission San Jose from 1836-1840. The Vallejos were leaders among Spanish pioneers. The small adobe, made of thick mud and straw walls, was used as sleeping quarters by Vallejo's ranch hands. Much of the building is reconstructed, some of it with pieces from the original structure.

9
Family
Restaurants

What Napoleon said about his army is equally true about families: they travel on their stomachs. Every excursion is brightened by a little snack at the right time, or a meal when the travelers are getting grumpy. And being prepared is the best way to ensure that mealtimes are a pleasant break in your day of touring and having fun.

There are hundreds of restaurants throughout the Santa Clara Valley — and lots of them welcome children. Many of them are family-run, and know that when you come in to eat with children in tow, you require different treatment than a table of adults. That understanding was the criteria for choosing the items in this list. In this chapter you'll find an alphabetical listing of some of the restaurants around the San Jose area that understand what kids need, what they like, and — maybe most important — what their parents appreciate when eating out with the kids.

Of course, restaurants come and go, names change, buildings disappear. This is a general guide; call first to be sure the information is still accurate. And as you get the hang of what to look for, you're sure to find lots of others that we didn't mention.

And keep in mind that prices are up-to-date as of this printing; they'll certainly change.

Happy hunting — and bon appétit!

✴ Armadillo Willy's

995 Saratoga Av. ✴ 255-7427
102355 DeAnza Bd., Cupertino ✴ 252-7427
1031 North San Antonio Rd., Los Altos ✴ (415) 941-2922
2624 Homestead Rd., Santa Clara ✴ 247-1100

Barbecue is the specialty at this nice, clean place where kids and adults alike can enjoy some very reasonably priced chicken and baby-back-ribs. Kids' meals start at only $1.99 and the adult menu items range from $4.95 to $13.95. Bibs and hand wipes are free.

✴ Baker's Square Restaurant and Pie Shop

5055 Almaden Expressway ✴ 267-6760
174 West Calaveras Bd., Milpitas ✴ 262-4683

2910 El Camino Real, Santa Clara ✳ *984-5433*
800 Ahwanee Av., Sunnyvale ✳ *736-6144*

Traditional American food and delicious baked goods to eat here or take away. Lunches — burgers or sandwiches — cost between $5 and $7, and complete dinners range between $7.25 and $11. Children's meals are smaller portions and prices, with high chairs and booster seats available. They don't have any birthday specials, but they will put a candle in your dessert and sing to you.

✳ Bullwinkle's Family Food 'n' Fun Restaurant

777 Lawrence Expressway, Santa Clara ✳ *249-4666*

More than just pizza and a very decent salad bar. Kids can run around here and play a variety of games. Tokens are given with each food purchase (extra tokens are available for purchase). Tickets are dispensed from the machines as your children play and can later be redeemed for prizes. A large mechanical Bullwinkle the moose and Rocky the squirrel sing along to loud music for entertainment. Popular for birthday parties, so plan to make a reservation well in advance.

✳ Chevy's

5305 Almaden Expressway ✳ *266-1815*
550 Winchester Bd. ✳ *241-0158*
204 Mathilda Av., Sunnyvale ✳ *737-7395*

If your brood enjoys Mexican food, this place will please both young and old. The first thing the kids notice is "El Machino," the tortilla-maker. Mine can stand and watch it work as long as it takes Mom or Dad to finish dinner.

Special kids' meals, which start at about $2.95, come in a basket and contain lots of small items (like a section of an ear of corn, a piece of melon, chips, etc. to go with the flauta, taco, cheeseburger or more); the pickiest eater will find something to fill up on. All Kiddie meals come with a Kiddie Cone of ice cream. You can pay between $6.95-$13.95 for an adult dinner, also filling and delicious.

But after the meal comes the real treat: the tour of the kitchen. Kids enjoy seeing all the machines at work making the fresh food, and stepping into the freezer. The best part is the machine that produces the little blobs of masa (cornmeal flour) that will become tortillas. Tours are always available to customers, but be reasonable: if it's Friday night, they may ask you to come back at a slower time so they can devote the time necessary to show you around.

For birthdays, the staff will come sing to you at your table, and you'll leave with a huge Mexican sombrero to remember the day by.

✸ Chuck E. Cheese Pizza

2445 Fontaine Rd. ✸ *238-9110*
1371 Kooser Rd. ✸ *267-8600*

A great place to play, although not necessarily to eat. Some kids get too wound up here to sit and eat a whole meal. Mechanized, singing creatures, waving flags, video monitors blaring, and games, games, games! (And noise, noise, noise!) You get tokens with each food purchase, for use in the games and rides (extra tokens can be purchased). Tickets earned by playing can be redeemed for gifts. Pizzas are competitively priced, free refills on drinks. Birthday parties. Not a peaceful place for a meal, but lots of fun.

✸ Coco's Family Restaurant

1753 North 1st St. ✸ *453-5030*
370 Kiely Bd., Santa Clara ✸ *244-3289*

Traditional American food for reasonable prices. Coco's has a Child's Menu that offers small-portion meals between $1.99-$2.85, and for bigger people, a full dinner can range from $5-about $10. Nothing fancy, just plain good food.

✸ Country Harvest Buffet

420 North Capital Av. ✸ *254-7740*
4067 Fremont Hub, Fremont ✸ *(510) 745-8833*
2670 El Camino Real, Santa Clara ✸ *247-9001*

You can't beat their prices for kids. Just $.45 per year of age through age 10 for lunch, and $.49 per year for dinner. Adults can eat for under $7.00 for breakfast, lunch and dinner. All meals include all-you-can-eat salad bar, beverages, bread and dessert. The meal itself consists of a large variety of main course items from any of five buffets. Menu items vary by day of the week. Some of the choices include roast beef and potatoes, all-you-can-eat shrimp, barbecued ribs or baked lasagna.

✸ Croutons

10100 South DeAnza Bd., Cupertino ✸ *253-6647*

An all-you-can-eat salad bar with more than 50 items to choose from, at least 5 homemade soups, fresh baked breads and fabulous muffins. And if you still have space, they have a dessert bar.

✳ Fresh Choice

1600 Saratoga Av. ✳ 866-1491
5353 Almaden Expressway ✳ 723-7991
1654 South Bascom Av., Campbell ✳ 559-1912
10123 North Wolf Rd., Cupertino ✳ 253-1605
555 East Calaveras Bd., Milpitas ✳ 262-6604
3041 Stevens Creek Bd., Santa Clara ✳ 243-7402

Strategically located at the entrance to most of our major shopping centers, Fresh Choice offers a spectacular all-you-can-eat salad bar with a great selection. Kids love the extra goodies which include: pizza, pasta, soups, breads, and a complete dessert bar with ice cream cones (all of which are included with the salad bar). The lines move quickly and the service is excellent.

✳ Good Earth Restaurant and Bakery

20807 Stevens Creek Bd., Cupertino ✳ 252-3555
206 North Santa Cruz Av., Los Gatos ✳ 395-6868
185 University Av., Palo Alto ✳ (415) 321-9449
2705 The Alameda, Santa Clara ✳ 984-0960

Good food <u>and</u> good for you! The Good Earth proves that healthful food can be delicious. All of their bread and rolls are ten-grain; even their desserts are healthful — yogurts, fresh fruit shakes (with high protein powder, on request), pumpkin walnut bread and more. Delicious, wholesome soup for $2.25 or $2.95; soup and one of their magnificent salads make a copious meal. Full dinners range from $7.25 to $9.95, sandwiches start at $5.45, and for kids 12 and under, there are about 11 smaller-portion meals to choose from, for $1.95-$3.55 (plus crayons and kid's menus to color). Their fish specials are a good deal.

✳ Happi House Restaurant

5353 Almaden Expressway ✳ 265-8282
3015 McKee Rd. ✳ 923-2120
397 Saratoga Av. ✳ 984-4806
695 North 5th St. ✳ 295-5554
1080 South Saratoga-Sunnyvale Rd. ✳ 253-4007

Japanese food the kids will love. These restaurants are easy to spot with their triangular A-frame roofs. And before you see them, you can often smell the delicious teriyaki seasoning. Happi House specialties are teriyaki combinations with your choice of chicken, beef or pork, a salad and rice. Kids' meals come with rice candy. All kids' combos are $2.79, and adult combos range from $4.85 to $5.85. You might also want to try the Oriental chicken salad.

✹ International House of Pancakes

644 North 1st St. ✹ 294-4130
5403 Stevens Creek Bd. ✹ 996-3393

If your kids enjoy pancakes, you have to try this. But IHOP isn't only for breakfast — although their breakfast is a good deal, at $2.99 for pancakes, eggs, and bacon or sausage. You can get a full family-style dinner, choice of turkey, pot roast, chicken or fried chicken plus side dishes, for $4.99.

✹ Just Breakfast

2901 Monterey Rd. ✹ 225-7631
3590 Homestead Av., Santa Clara ✹ 247-2753

Despite the name, you can get breakfast or lunch here too — but as you can guess, breakfast are their specialty. Omelettes and eggs fixed just about every way you can imagine are menu favorites. Kids can eat for just under $3.00, and adult breakfasts are all under $7.00.

✹ Kirk's Steakburgers

2388 South Bascom Av., Campbell ✹ 371-3565
361 California Av., Palo Alto ✹ (415) 326-6159
844 East El Camino Real, Sunnyvale ✹ 732-5475
1330 Saratoga-Sunnyvale Rd., Sunnyvale ✹ 446-2988

Their Ground Steakburger is just a fancy name for hamburgers, but these are are very lean and very big. A few of the most popular are the Cheddar Cheese Steakburger with or without the works, and the Griller Steakburger with grilled onions and Swiss cheese.

✹ Marie Callendar's

620 Blossom Hill Rd. ✹ 578-0643
2831 Meridian Av. ✹ 265-7130
780 Winchester Bd. ✹ 243-9018
20750 Stevens Creek Bd., Cupertino ✹ 255-2317
333 South Abbott Av., Milpitas ✹ 263-7437
18599 Sutter Bd., Morgan Hill ✹ 778-7373

Home-style cooking includes freshly-baked pies and home-made entrees (just like Mom would make if she had more time). The portions are generous. Kids' meals offer a choice from spaghetti, macaroni and cheese, soup and salad bar and, if all else fails, grilled cheese and hamburgers. All kids' menu items are $2.49. The most popular adult items are the Chicken Pot Pie and the Chicken Sesame Salad. Adult items start at $7.95.

✳ Old Spaghetti Factory
51 North San Pedro ✳ 288-7488

Kids, kids, kids — you see lots of 'em here! Designed to resemble a train station, there are even a couple of trolley cars you can eat in. The decor is turn-of-the-century, and the dark wood is off-set by antiques. But it isn't as expensive as it looks. You can buy dinner for a family of four for about $25-$30 and up, without extras like cocktails or desserts.

They have special children's menus for lunch and dinner, with small portions, for $2.95-$3.75. Good, traditional Italian and American food. But if you don't enjoy waiting, don't come here on a Friday night; the crowd backs up at the door and you can wait between a half-hour and an hour, or more.

✳ The Original Hickory Pit
989 East Campbell Av., Campbell ✳ 371-2400
39410 Fremont Bd., Fremont ✳ (510) 790-1992
2310 Homestead Rd., Los Altos ✳ 720-8733

Famous for their barbecue meats, fresh-made pies and huge breakfasts, the Original Hickory Pit is the place for big eaters. All meats are smoked over a huge hickory-chip-filled pit. The flavor is out of this world.

✳ Pizzeria Uno
19930 Stevens Creek Bd., Cupertino ✳ 973-1466
2570 El Camino Real, Santa Clara ✳ 241-5152

A very upscale pizza parlor. If the kids really want pizza but you'd like something a little different, you can order them a small individual pizza for just $3.29 while you enjoy a specialty salad, tortellini or lasagna. Adult items range from $6.00 to $10.00.

✳ Red Lobster

2040 Aborn Rd. ✳ 274-2400
5343 Almaden Expressway ✳ 266-9275
39401 Fremont Bd., Fremont ✳ (510) 657-2436
503 East Calaveras Bd., Milpitas ✳ 942-0781

Kids who might not usually eat fish just might try it here. They have kid-sized portions of popcorn shrimp, chicken tenders or fried shrimp. Each kids' entree is served with French fries or cheese sticks. Other specialties include fish, Maine lobster, shrimp, crab and lots of other seafood items. Kids' entrees are all under $4.00, and adult entrees start at $9.99.

✳ Sizzler Family Restaurant

Many locations throughout the Santa Clara Valley.

This place packs in the kids. Their Buffet Court (all-you-can-eat salad and dessert bars) has something for everyone, and kids enjoy making their own tacos, salads (including fruits in season) and yummy desserts (cakes, ice cream they pump themselves and all sorts of toppings). Some locations offer an additional mini kids' salad bar complete with fries, chicken fingers, and Jello. Lunch prices start at about $1.99 for a kid's meal: burger and potato of your choice. Steak lunch starts at about $4.99. For dinner they have all kinds of chicken, steak and combinations of steak with seafood, starting at about $6.99, and you can get a kid's meal for about $1.99.

They offer a copious, reasonable, Sunday brunch with pancakes, waffles, eggs, toast, just about everything kids dream of for breakfast or brunch, $3.99 for kids 10 and under, $6.99 for adults. And they don't mind if toddlers share from Mom's or Dad's plate. They'll even sing to you on your birthday, and to top off the meal in the right mood, they bring you lollipops for the kids. There are always lot of kids, and most give this place two thumbs up.

✳ Strings, the Pasta Place

1554 Saratoga Av. ✳ 866-0766
20735 Stevens Creek Bd., Cupertino ✳ 257-5666
481 East Calaveras Bd., Milpitas ✳ 263-2332

What kid doesn't like pasta of one sort or another? Their Kids' Menu offers a choice of pastas with a pick-your-own sauce (on top, or on the side) for $1.95, or a small cheese pizza for $2.95. For adults, prices range from about $5.50 for spaghetti, to about $8.95 for the usual assortment of Italian favorites. Their desserts and ice creams were a little too exotic for my small diners' palates, but the balloons made up for it.

✳ Swenson's

162 Oakridge Mall ✳ 578-1971
1779 Hillsdale Av. ✳ 266-0992
300 El Paseo Shopping Center ✳ 374-4420
119 The Pruneyard, Campbell ✳ 971-3737
20 South Santa Cruz Av., Los Gatos ✳ 395-5900

You can watch them make their own delicious ice cream at the Oakridge location (twice a week). Sandwiches, soups and salads are the primary menu items. Picky eaters can always get a hot dog or grilled cheese sandwich. Top off your lunch with one of over 40 flavors of fresh ice cream, or you might want to try one of their special desserts, such as the Hot Fudge Bonanza Split with a whole banana, one and a half scoops of ice cream, hot fudge, whipped cream, a cherry and a Swenson's wafer.

10
Resources

Convention and Visitors Bureaus & Chambers of Commerce

This listing includes the greater San Jose/Santa Clara Valley region as well as places listed under Chapter 7, Day Trips.

APTOS Chamber of Commerce
9099 Soquel Dr., #12, Aptos 95003 ✹ 688-1467

CAMPBELL Chamber of Commerce
1628 W. Campbell Av., Campbell 95008-1535 ✹ 378-6252

CAPITOLA Chamber of Commerce
621 B Capitola Av., Capitola 94010 ✹ 475-6522

CASTROVILLE Chamber of Commerce
Box 744, Castroville 94012 ✹ 633-2465

CUPERTINO Chamber of Commerce
20455 Silverado Ave., Cupertino 94014 ✹ 252-7054

FREMONT Chamber of Commerce
2201 Walnut Av., Fremont 94538 ✹ (510) 795-2244

GILROY Chamber of Commerce
7471 Monterey St., Gilroy 95020 ✹ 842-6437

GILROY Visitors Bureau
7780 Monterey St., Gilroy 95020 ✹ 842-6436

MILPITAS Chamber of Commerce
75 S. Milpitas Bd., Milpitas ✹ 262-2613

MORGAN HILL Chamber of Commerce
Box 786, Morgan Hill 95038 ✹ 779-9444

MOSS LANDING Chamber of Commerce
Box 41, Moss Landing 94039 ✹ 633-5202

MOUNTAIN VIEW Chamber of Commerce
580 Castro St., Mountain View 94041 ✹ (415) 968-8378

PALO ALTO Chamber of Commerce
325 Forest Av., Palo Alto 94301 ✹ (415) 324-3121

PAJARO VALLEY Chamber of Commerce
Box 1748, Watsonville 95077 ✹ 724-3900

SALINAS Chamber of Commerce
119 E. Alisal St., Salinas 93902 ✳ 424-7611

SAN JOSE Convention and Visitors Bureau
333 W. San Carlos St., San Jose 94110 ✳ 295-9600

SAN JOSE Visitor Information Center
150 W. San Carlos St., San Jose 95110 ✳ 283-8833

SAN MATEO County Convention and Visitors Bureau
111 Anza Bd., #410, Burlingame 94010 ✳ (415) 348-7600

SANTA CLARA Convention & Visitors Bureau
2200 Laurelwood Rd., Santa Clara ✳ 296-7111
1515 El Camino Real ✳ 296-7111

SANTA CRUZ County convention and Visitor Bureau
701 Front St., Santa Cruz 95060 ✳ 425-1234/(800) 833-3494

SARATOGA Chamber of Commerce
20460 Saratoga-Los Gatos Rd., Saratoga 95070 ✳ 867-0753

SOQUEL Chamber of Commerce
4640 Soquel Dr., Soquel 95073 ✳ 476-3338

SOLEDAD Chamber of Commerce
248 Main St., Soledad 93960 ✳ 678-1936

SUNNYVALE Chamber of Commerce
499 S. Murphy Av., Sunnyvale 94086 ✳ 736-4971

WATSONVILLE Area Chamber of Commerce
Box 470, Watsonville 95077 ✳ 724-3849

Top 20 Places to Go in the San Jose Area

Alum Rock Park
Casa de Fruta
Center for the Performing Arts
Children's Discovery Museum
Christmas in the Park
Egyptian Museum and Planetarium

Happy Hollow Park and Zoo
Martin Luther King Library
Mission Santa Clara & Santa Clara
    University Campus
Paramount's Great America
Raging Waters
Roaring Camp Railroad
San Jose Giants Baseball
San Jose Historical Museum
San Jose Museum of Art
San Jose Sharks Game
Santa Cruz Beach Boardwalk
The Tech Museum of Innovation
Vasona Park and River Walk
Winchester Mystery House

Free Activities/Outings
for Families

Art Galleries
Bike Riding
Bookstores
Farmer's Markets
Hotel Hopping
Los Gatos Creek Trail Walk
Nurseries
Parades
Parks
Pet Shops
Playgrounds
Public Libraries
St. Joseph Cathedral
San Jose Airport
Shopping Malls
Toy Stores

Birthday Party Ideas

Action Zone – Indoor Paintball Center, 111 Uranium Drive, Unit A, 738-2255. In this huge indoor 3-story building, kids can run around and shoot each other with paint pellets. It doesn't stain but parents will probably want them to wear old clothes. They can experience a fog-filled maze, a 50-foot slide, target and spectator areas. There are also video and pinball games in a separate arcade. The party package includes two hours of play and 200 rounds of ammo, $125 for five players, $205 for ten.

Astro Jump 292-7876. You've seen these fun toys before at special events, parks and playgrounds. Now you can get one for your backyard. These inflatable animals, dinosaurs and castles provide the perfect safe and enclosed area for your little party-goers to jump around. Prices start at $125 for a half day and include set-up and tear-down.

Children's Discovery Museum. 180 Woz Way, San Jose 298-5437 ext. 259. For just $12 per child and $5 per adult you can enjoy one and one-half hours in the Museum, pizza, soda, a prize bag for each child, a reserved party area and the birthday child gets two free passes to return to the Museum. (Members receive a special reduced rate).

Chuck E. Cheese, 2445 Fontaine Road, San Jose (238-9110) and 1371 Kooser Road, San Jose (267-8600). You get a reserved table(s) with balloons and paper goods, pizza, soda and a few game tokens for each party-goer, all for $6.49 per child.

Circus Soozee 298-7739. She'll perform a mini-circus at your party complete with popcorn and performing poodle. She will juggle, perform magic tricks, unicycle, make balloon animals and get the audience involved. Parties cost $150 for an hour.

Eastridge Ice Arena, 2190-A Tully Road, San Jose 238-0440. They offer a great deal at $5 per child ($2 off the regular admission) for skates and skating time. If you have seven or more participants the birthday person skates for free. They will also provide a room for you to decorate and have the party in.

Golden State Roller Palace, 397 Blossom Hill Road 226-1156. For just $6.25 per child each receives admission, skate rental, ice cream, a cup cake, soda, and the birthday child gets two 2-for-1 passes. For $7.75 they get all of the above and a glow-light.

Gymboree, 243-7812 Seven in Santa Clara County, call for the location closest to you. A great idea for the little ones ages 0-5. Children can enjoy structured play time which includes singing, parachute games, play equipment. The party is led by an instructor so parents can participate and leave everything up to them. The best part is, they clean up the mess. The Party Package prices vary by location.

Happy Hollow Park and Zoo, 1300 Senter Road, San Jose 295-8383 (see Chapter 3, Parks). You could easily spend the day at this amusement part and zoo. Admission is normally $4.00 but with twelve or more they will discount the admission $.50 per person. Picnic areas are available for $10 for up to three hours. You can purchase a food package for $6.00 per person which includes hot dog, chips, small drink and an ice cream, or you can bring your own. The rides are an additional fee but they have a great free puppet show on the weekends.

Malibu Grand Prix, 340 Blomquist Road, Redwood City (415) 366-6463. A little of a drive but well worth it. Your little road warriors will be thrilled. They have two complete race tracks where kids can race against the clock in real go-cart/race cars. Great fun for children 4½ feet and up. Party package includes three laps around the track for each child, eight game tokens, a reserved table for one hour, enough pizza to feed six, and a pitcher of soda. If you want to make a day of it you can also step next door to Malibu Castle to play miniature golf and more video games.

My Party Pony & Petting Zoo 847-6424. Features live ponies for petting, riding and photos. They also provide additional small barnyard animals for an additional fee so kids can enjoy a mini petting zoo.

Planet Granite, 2901 Mead Avenue, Santa Clara 727-2777. For $100 for five kids, you get 2 hours of climbing with the assistance of an instructor, rental gear (shoes and a harness), a room to decorate and celebrate in (bring your own goodies). $20 for each additional kid.

Scoops N Toobes, 6148 Bollinger Road, Cupertino, 255-1151. Lots of indoor space and equipment to climb, crawl, jump and play. Adventurous parents can join in as well; knee pads provided. Party package includes a meal of hot dog or pizza, chips, punch and all of the playing you can handle. Bring your own cake.

Sheraton Hotel, 1801 Barber Lane Milpitas, 943-0600. A unique idea which Mom and Dad will also enjoy. For $139.00, your child can bring three friends to camp out in the living room of a Tower Suite, while mom and dad get their own private room. The kids bring their own sleeping bags and can stay up late while mom and dad relax. The package includes the suite, a birthday cake, balloons, soft drinks, pizza and unlimited swimming.

Snapdragon Puppet Productions (415) 578-1725. For a reasonable fee of $150 Snap the smoke-breathing dragon will delight your birthday kid with interactive fairy tales and imaginative stories. He brings his own stage, sound system, curtains and lights.

Winchester Mystery House, 525 S. Winchester Bd., 247-2101. The birthday girl or boy becomes Honorary Tour Guide and gets to help the actual tour guide. After the tour, enjoy a cake and drink, plus a special treat for the guest of honor. They set up and clean up; party lasts an hour. $10.95 per child, up to 2 adults admitted for child price. Additional adults $15.95.

YMCA Indoor-Swim Party, 13500 Quito Road, Saratoga 370-1877. The Southwest YMCA provides swim time with lifeguard supervision. A great idea for summer or winter birthdays. Birthday packages cost $100 for 10 children if you bring your own food, drinks and cake, and $150 if you'd like them to provide it. Either way they will set up and clean up.

Other Suggestions:
   Bowling
   Children's Theater
   Fast-food restaurants also offer birthday packages
   Fishing
   Hiking Trails
   Light rail across town to a movie and back
   Paramounts Great America
   Parks
   Rhinos Roller Hockey Game
   Roaring Camp Railroad
   Santa Cruz Beach Boardwalk
   Sharks Ice Hockey Game
   Ventriloquist

Rainy Weather Ideas

Art Galleries
Bookstores
Bowling
Children's Discovery Museum
Concerts
Hobby Stores
Hotel Hopping
Humane Society
Ice Skating
Libraries
Pet Stores
Public Libraries
Roller Skating
Shopping Malls
Sporting Events
Tours of the Working World
Toy Stores
Winchester Mystery House

Summer Classes, Workshops, Programs and Camps for Children

You or your children can learn to swim, do crafts, act, sing, play music, dance — just about anything you can think of — somewhere around the San Jose/Santa Clara Valley area. On a local level, call the **Parks & Recreation** district (see the white pages of the telephone directory for your county) to receive their announcements of summer programs. Local **schools** and **religious centers** also offer summer classes and workshops, as do many community centers. For a free **Camp Directory**, contact the American Camping Association, P.O. Box 151493,

San Rafael, Ca 94915; 1 (800) 362-2236. Also check the **YMCA/YWCA;** they have camps in Boulder Creek, Cupertino, Morgan Hill, Milpitas, San Jose (3 centers) and Saratoga; call for more information. Some camps welcome children and parents together, like the **San Jose Family Camp** (277-4666). And don't forget to check the family publications, like the Bay Area Parent, for more listings. Besides the general outdoor-fun camps, check the following list for a sampling of specialized camps where children can learn while they have fun.

Arts (creative or performing)

Whichever creative arts your child enjoys or wants to learn, you'll find a camp for it somewhere in the region. Check the Yellow Pages under the appropriate area (Dance, Piano, Music, etc.).

The **San Jose Museum of Art,** 110 S. Market St. offers art classes for all ages, taught by practicing artists.

Children's Creative Learning Centers

These three campuses operate year-round, but deserve mention here as a summer option. Cupertino/Los Altos area (age 2-5) – 736-7334; Stanford/Palo Alto area (age 5-12) – (415)493-6006; Sunnyvale/Santa Clara area (infant-5) – 932-2288

Computers/Science

Check with the colleges and universities in the area for their residential and day program computer camps, as well as the following partial list:

FutureKids, 6531 Crown Bd., Ste., 3B, San Jose (997-8909) and 383 Jacklin Rd., Milpitas (934-1943)

Pine Hill School, 1975 Cambrianna Dr., San Jose (371-5881)

Santa Clara University Computer Camp (554-4900)

Tech Museum of Innovation, 145 W. San Carlos St., San Jose (279-7150)

Day Camps

See Camp Directory, above, or check the categories in this listing for the type of day camp your child is interested in. Also check with the regional parks and wilderness areas for special seasonal day camps.

Girl Scouts of Santa Clara County

Girl Scouts offer many summer adventures for girls, such as resident camps or daily day camps. For information and registration, call the Girl Scout Council at (408)287-4170 or (415)968-8396.

Sports

Whatever sport your youngsters enjoy, they can do it during the summer somewhere in the region. The California Sports Center, 3800 Blackford Ave., Suite C, San Jose (246-7795) offers families training in just about any sport. Here's a smattering of what's available; for more, check the Yellow Pages under the sport. Also check with local high schools, churches, Parks & Recreation districts, etc.

Gymnastics

Kids who love to climb the walls may find what they're looking for in a gymnastics class. Here are a few; for more, see Gymnastics Instruction in the Yellow Pages. Also check with local colleges or universities.

Airborne Gymnastics, 2240 Martin Ave., Santa Clara (970-8411)

California Gymnastics Center, 336 Race St., San Jose (280-KIDS; 280-5437)

California Sports Center, 3800 Blackford Ave., San Jose (246-7795)

Santa Clara Valley Gymnastics Club, 690 E. Calaveras Bd., Milpitas (946-6607)

Taylor's Acro-Gymnastics, 401 Jackson, San Jose (295-2276)

West Valley Gymnastics School, 1190 Dell Ave., Unit I, Campbell (374-8692)

Horseback Riding

Many stables throughout the Santa Clara Valley region offer summer programs for children, where they can learn to ride and to take care of their horse. Here's a partial listing; for more information, see the Yellow Pages under Horse Stables or Riding Academies.

Calero Ranch Stables, 23201 McKean Rd.,San Jose (268-2567)

Alum Rock Stable, 16235 Alum Rock Ave., San Jose (251-8800

Full House Farm, Lost Altos Hills (415/948-2530)

Rosebank Equestrian Center, 17103 Hicks Rd., Los Gatos (415/988-1508)

Chaparral Ranch, 3375 Calaveras Rd., Milpitas (263-3336)

Besides classes, you and your children can find special horseback rides scheduled through the many regional parks. Del Valle Regional Park (7000 Del Valle Rd., Pleasanton 94550; (510) 373-0332) and Sunol-Ohlone Regional Wilderness (P.O. Box 82, Sunol 94586; (510) 862-2244) both have scheduled rides at different times of year. Call for information.

Martial Arts

Many academies in the area offer special summer programs. Check the Yellow Pages under Martial Arts.

Math

Kumon Educational Institute has many centers throughout the Santa Clara area (1/800/999-MATH)

Learning Plus (354-4438)

Sylvan Learning Center, San Jose (257-2740) and Cupertino (446-3623)

Minigym, 4115 Jackson Drive. Summer "Exploragym" day camp for kids 3-7 (559-4616)

Swimming/Aquatics

Almaden Valley Athletic Club Swim School, 5400 Camden Av., San Jose (267-4032)

Santa Clara Synchronized Swimming Club, Santa Clara (243-9311)

Water Babies Swim School, 973 Apricot, Campbell (377-4626)

West Coast Aquatics, P.O. Box 32188, San Jose (259-4522)

Also check Parks & Recreation districts and college campuses for summer swim programs.

Theater

Bay Area Shakespeare Camps, taught by the San Francisco Shakespeare Theater, offer kids the chance to meet the Bard and learn about all the theater arts, as well as performing. Sites vary for this 2-week program. (415/666-2313 or 800/978-PLAY)

California Theatre Center offers Summer Theatre Conservatories for ages 8 to 18. Learn from professional actors and teachers; performances at the end of the sessions. Various sites. (245-2979).

Children's Playhouse of San Jose may be right for the kids who love an audience. 285 Blossom Hill Rd., in the Oak Grove High School Theater (578-PLAY).

Palo Alto Children's Theater does summer stock theater, age 8-18, which gives several performances at the end of each session, and a series of summer classes for ages 8-10 and 10-high school. (415/329-2216) or (415/329-26510

San Jose Children's Musical Theater offers an intensive 3-week summer program called the Conservatory of Performing Arts (COPA) where youngsters can learn voice, drama, dance as well as the variety arts (stage make-up, combat, etc.). The largest children's theater in the U.S. where kids perform for kids. Two summer sessions, one in June and one in July/August. Call for locations of classes. 753 N. 9th Street, Suite 135 (288-5437)

Santa Clara Junior Theater offers a special summer conservatory, where kids can learn to sing, act and perform. 27 years old and going strong. 969 Kiely Bd., Santa Clara (244-7258).

(For more information on the above, see Chapter 4, Performing Arts.)

Wilderness Skills

Many of the regional parks and wilderness areas offer summer workshops where kids can gain outdoor skills and acquire knowledge about the region we live in. For example, from spring through summer the Sunol-Ohlone Regional Wilderness program called Wilderness Explorers will introduce your kids to the wilder side of the region, or they can learn about nature and the indigenous people who lived here for centuries before the Europeans in the Junior Naturalist Academy or the Native American Studies programs at Coyote Hills Regional Park. See Chapter 3, Parks.

FOR KIDS WITH SPECIAL NEEDS

Creativity Unlimited of Santa Clara, *1403 Parkmoor Avenue, San Jose* ✴ *288-8189*

Parents Helping Parents-Children With Special Needs, *3041 Olcott, Santa Clara* ✴ *727-5773*

Connie Brown & Associates, *280 E. Hamilton Avenue, Campbell* ✴ *370-9562*

They specialize in the evaluation and treatment of childrens' speech and language problems in children.

Crippled Children's Society of Santa Clara, *1515 Franklin Street, Santa Clara* ✴ *554-9591*

Deaf Counseling Advocacy & Referral Agency ✹ *298-6770*

Hope Rehabilitation Service, *4351 Lafayette Street, Santa Clara* ✹ *748-2850*

United Cerebral Palsy Association of Santa Clara, *480 San Antonio Road, Mountain View* ✹ *(415) 279-8987*

United Way of Santa Clara County, *1922 The Alameda, San Jose* ✹ *247-1200*

Dyslexia Treatment & Counseling Center, *940 Saratoga Avenue, San Jose* ✹ *2421-3330*

The Morgan Center, *201 Covington Avenue, Los Altos* ✹ *(415) 948-6834*
Specializing in the individual assessment, teaching and training of autistic and brain-injured children.

The Stanbridge Academy, *890 Pomeroy Avenue, Santa Clara* ✹ *261-6610*
Educational programs for children with verbal and non-verbal learning disabilities, including Attention Deficit Disorder.

Education & Therapy Associates, *15100 Los Gatos Boulevard, Los Gatos* ✹ *356-7603*
They specialize in treating children with speech and language disorders.

PHP The Family Resource Center, *535 Race Street #140, San Jose* ✹ *288-5010*
A resource center for the families with special needs. They provide access to comprehensive resource information by telephone, mail and computer modem.

The Diabetes Society, *1165 Lincoln Avenue, #300, San Jose* ✹ *287-3785*
Offering special classes, support groups, free screenings, consultations and a family camp.

PUBLICATIONS

The Argus, 3850 Decoto Rd., Fremont ✹ (510) 794-0111

Bay Area Parent, 401-A Alberto Way, Los Gatos 95032 ✹ 358-1414

Business Journal, 96 N. Third St., Suite 100, San Jose 95112 ✹ 295-3800

Campbell Express/Cambrian News, 334 E. Campbell Av., Campbell 95008 ✳ 374-9700

Cupertino Courier, 10501 S. DeAnza Bd., Cupertino 95014 ✳ 255-7500

The Dispatch, 4400 Monterey Rd., Gilroy 95021-2365 ✳ 842-6411

Jewish Community News, 14855 Oka Rd., Los Gatos 95030 ✳ 358-3033

Kids, Kids, Kids, 455 Los Gatos Bd., Los Gatos 95030 ✳ 358-1414

Los Altos Town Crier, 138 Main St., Los Altos 94022 ✳ (415) 948-4489

Los Gatos Weekly Times, 245 Almendra Av., Los Gatos 95030 ✳ 354-3110

Metro, 550 S. 1st St., San Jose 95113-2815 ✳ 298-8000

Milpitas Post, 11615-A S. Main St., Milpitas 95035 ✳ 262-2454

Morgan Hill Times, 30 East 3rd St., Morgan Hill 95037 ✳ 779-4106

El Observador, P.O. Box 1990, San Jose 95109 ✳ 295-4272

Palo Alto Weekly, P.O. Box 1610, Palo Alto 94302 ✳ (415) 326-8216

San Jose City Times, 550 S. 1st St., San Jose 95113-2815 ✳ 298-8000

San Jose Mercury Times, 750 Ridder Park Dr., San Jose 95190 ✳ 920-5000

Santa Clara Valley Weekly, P.O. Box 755, Santa Clara 95052-0755 ✳ 243-2000

Saratoga News, 1437 Saratoga Av., Suite E-2, Saratoga 95070 ✳ 867-6397

Senior Times, 42 E. Santa Clara St., Suite 213, San Jose 95113 ✳ 288-5771

South Bay Accent, 4300 Stevens Creek Bd., San Jose 95129 ✳ 244-5100

COLLEGES AND UNIVERSITIES

California College of Arts and Crafts, Hayward

Chabot College, 25555 Hesperian Bd., Hayward 94545 ✳ (510) 786-6000

California State University, Hayward, 25800 Carlos Bee Bd., Hayward ✹ (510) 881-3000

Cañada College, 4200 Farm Hill Bd., Redwood City 94061 ✹ (415) 306-3100

College of San Mateo, 1700 W. Hillsdale Bd., San Mateo 94402 ✹ (415) 574-6161

DeAnza Community College, 21250 Stevens Creek Bd., Cupertino ✹ 996-4814

Evergreen Valley College, 3095 Yerba Buena Rd., San Jose 95135 (San Jose-Evergreen Community College District.) ✹ 274-7900

Foothill College, 12345 El Monte Rd., Los Altos Hills 94022 ✹ 960-4334
    Also **Middlefield Campus**, 4000 Middlefield Rd., Palo Alto 94303 ✹ (415) 424-8600

Gavilan College, 5055 Santa Teresa Bd., Gilroy 95020 ✹ 847-1400

Hartnell College, 156 Homestead Ave., Salinas 93901 ✹ 755-6700

Las Positas College, 3033 Collier Canyon Rd., Livermore 94550 ✹ (510) 373-5800

Ohlone College, 43600 Mision Bd., Fremont 94539 ✹ (510) 659-6000

San Jose City College, 2100 Moorpark Av. ✹ 298-2181 (San Jose-Evergreen Community College District)

San Jose State University, One Washington Square, San Jose ✹ 924-1000. California's oldest public higher education institution.

Santa Clara University, 500 El Camino Real, Santa Clara ✹ 554-4754

Skyline College, 3300 College Dr., San Bruno 94066 ✹ 738-4100

University of California at Santa Cruz, 1156 High St., Santa Cruz 95064 ✹ 459-2131

West Valley College, 14000 Fruitvale Av., Saratoga 95070 ✹ 867-2200

SPECIAL TELEPHONE NUMBERS

Ambulance, Fire, Police 911

American Heart Association 977-4950

Abducted-Abused-Exploited Children (800)248-8020

Al-Anon/Alateen for Families 379-1051

Alcoholism and Drug Dependence Hotline 267-4357

American Cancer Society 287-5973

American Diabetes Association 983-1288

American Lung Association 998-5864

American Red Cross 292-6242

Animal Control Santa Clara County 299-6100
>   emergencies 299-6749
>   information 299-6075

Bicycle licenses 277-4444

Boys Town National Hotline (800) 448-3000

California Missing Children Hotline (800) 222-3463

California State Automobile Association (AAA)
>   Oakridge 629-1911
>   Santa Clara 985-9300
>   Emergency Road Service – 24 hours (members) (800)400-4222

Catholic Diocese of San Jose 925-0100

Catholic Charities of Santa Clara County 944-0282

Catholic Youth Organization (CYO) 944-0776

Child Care Information & Assistance 947-0900

Child Quest International 492-1122

Children's Counseling Center of Catholic Charities 983-1004

Children's Home Society of California 475-3996

Children's Hospital at Stanford (Lucile Salter Packard Children's Hospital) (see Hospitals)

Community Centers (San Jose)
>   Administration – 333 W. Santa Clara 277-4661
>   Almaden – 6445 Camden Av. 268-1133
>   Berryesse – 14630 Noble Av. 272-3544

Branham Recreation & Aquatic Center (disabled) – 1750 Branham Ln. 265-0808

Camden Lifetime Activity Center – 3369 Union Ave. 559-8553

Evergreen – 4860 San Felipe Rd. 270-2220

Gardner – 520 W. Virginia Av. 279-1498

Hank Lopez – 1694 Adrian Way 251-2850

Kirk – 1601 Foxworthy Ave. 723-1571

Leininger – 1300 Senter Rd. 286-3626

Mayfair – 2039 Kammerer Av. 729-3475

Millbrook – 3200 Millbrook Dr. 274-1343

Northside – 488 N. 6th St. 275-1638

Olinder – 848 E. William 279-1138

Roosevelt – 901 E. Santa Clara 998-2223

Solari – 3590 Cas Dr. 224-0415

Southside – 5585 Cottle Rd. 629-3336

Starbird – 1050 Boynton Av. 984-1954

Watson – 1082 Jackson 280-7355

Willow Glen – 855 Pine Av. 269-4641

(For other areas, see City or County listings of White Pages)

Cystic Fibrosis Foundation-N. Cal. 293-9353

Deaf Blind Services 293-3323

Deaf Communications TDD (800) 342-5966

Family Service Association of Santa Clara 288-6200

Family Services Center 445-7700

Hemophilia Foundation of Northern California 568-6243

Hospitals

Alexian Brothers Hospital 259-5000

Cedar Ridge Hospital (mental health care for adolescents) 356-5788

El Camino Hospital, Mountain View (415) 940-7000

Good Samaritan Hospital 559-2011

Lucile Salter Packard Children's Hospital at Stanford 497-8000

Mision Oaks Hospital 356-4111

O'Connor Hospital 947-2500

Samaritan Medical Care Center 281-2772

San Jose Medical Center 998-3212

Santa Teresa Community Hospital 972-7000

Shriners Hospital for Crippled Children (415) 665-1100

Stanford University Hospital (415) 723-4000

Humane Society of Santa Clara Valley 727-3383

Jewish Family Services 356-7576

La Leche League of Northern California (415) 983-6525
Referral service 264-0994
Las Madres 265-4056
Make a Wish Foundation, Santa Clara Division 288-7877
March of Dimes, West Regional Office 292-1400
Medical assistance – emergency 911 (also see Hospitals)
National Runaway Switchboard (800) 621-4000
Nursing Mothers' Counsel (Palo Alto) 272-1448
Nursing Mothers' Resource 377-5350
Parent Effectiveness Training 268-5250
Parents Helping Parents 288-5010
Parents without Partners 227-5718
Milpitas 946-4273
Parks & Recreation District – see County listings in White Pages of
Telephone Directory
Santa Clara Police Athletic Gym 727-8118
Santa Clara Parents Co-op 248-5131
San Jose Regional Transit 277-4217
Santa Clara Regional Transit 321-2300
St. Jude Children's Research Hospital (800) 877-5833
Suicide & Crisis Service 279-3312
United Cerebral Palsy association of Santa Clara-San Mateo Counties,
Inc. 279-8987
United Way of Santa Clara County 247-1200
Information and Referral 248-4636
YMCA of Santa Clara Valley 298-3888
YWCA of Santa Clara Valley 295-4011
Youth Crisis Hotline (800) 448-4663
Youth Employment Service 998-4272
Youth Science Institute 272-1301

Recommended Reading

...for further exploration...

The following books were chosen because they contain information useful to families or people exploring the region with children. Each one is different; you'll find all sorts of interesting little tidbits. There are a lot of other guides, too; use this as a starter, and have fun making your own "favorite" list.

Adventuring in the San Francisco Bay Area. Peggy Wayburn. Sierra Club Books. 1995.

Along the King's Highway: The California Missions. Brian Bates. Multi-media materials for MacIntosh computers. Bates Productions, Fair Oaks, CA. 1995. (916) 962-1052.

Best Hikes with Children: San Francisco's South Bay. Bill McMillon and Kevin McMillon. The Mountaineers, Seattle, WA. 1992.

California Almanac. James S. Fay, Editor. Pacific Data Resources. 1993.

California with Kids. Frommer's Family Travel Guide. Prentice Hall Travel, New York. 3rd edition, 1994.

California's Great Outdoor Events. Ken McKowen. Foghorn Press, San Francisco, 1995.

Discover Historic California. George and Jan Roberts. Gem Guide Books Co, Pico Rivera, CA. 1988.

Fodor's Guide to Northern California. Daniel Mangin, Editor. San Francisco, CA. 1995.

Ghost Towns and Mining Camps of California: a History and Guide. Remi Nadeau. Crest Publishers, Santa Barbara, CA. 1992.

Guide to Silicon Valley. Leigh Weimers. Western Tanager Press, Santa Cruz, CA. 1993.

Kidding Around San Francisco. Rosemary Zibart. John Muir Publications, Santa Fe, NM. 1989.

Northern California Discovery Guide. Don & Betty Martin. Pine Cone Press, Columbia, Ca. 1993.

<u>1000 California Place Names</u>. Erwin G.Gudde. University of California Press, Berkeley, CA. 1959.

<u>Open to the Public: a Guide to the Museums of Northern California</u>. Charlene Akers. Heyday Books, Berkeley, CA. 1994.

<u>Places to Go with Children in Northern California</u>. Elizabeth Pomada. Chronicle Books, San Francisco, CA. 1993.

<u>Quick Escapes from San Francisco</u>. Karen Misuraca. The Globe Pequot Press, Old Saybrook, CT. 1993.

<u>San Francisco and Beyond: 101 Affordable Excursions</u>. Pamela P. Hegarty. Travel for Less Press, Hercules, CA. 1994.

<u>San Francisco with Kids</u>. Frommer's Family Travel Guide. Prentice Hall Travel, New York. 2nd edition, 1994.

<u>Santa Cruz Mountains Trail Book, The</u>. Tom Taber. The Oak Valley Press, San Mateo, CA. 1994.

INDEX

Ordering Information

To order additional copies of

please send your name, address, phone number and check or money order payable to:

Wordwrights International
P.O. Box 1941
Carmichael, CA 95609-1941

Each copy is $11.95 plus tax and shipping. For quantity/group discounts, please call (916) 483-4961.

Sales tax: California residents, please add sales tax.

Shipping/Handling: $2.00 for first book, 50¢ for each additional book. Allow 3 weeks for delivery.

Fundraising: San Jose with Kids is available to groups for fund-raising. Please call (916) 483-4961 for details.

Your satisfaction is guaranteed or your money promptly refunded.

Also available from Wordwrights International:

A Family Guide to the Greater Sacramento Region

A complete family resource to the Sacramento area, from the Valley to the mountains, including attractions, activities, sports & recreation, festivals, performing arts, day trips, Gold Country, wildlife viewing and much, much more!

Mastering the Basic Ingredients of English

An innovative recipe for English that puts *you* in charge of the kitchen! Forget rote memorization and complicated rules — now you can *understand* the English language better than you ever did in school!

To order the above books, send your name, address, phone number and check or money order payable to:

Wordwrights International
P.O. Box 1941
Carmichael, CA 95609-1941

Each copy is $9.95 plus tax and shipping. For quantity/group discounts, please call (916) 483-4961.

Sales tax: California residents, please add sales tax.

Shipping/Handling: $2.00 per book, plus 50c for each additional book. Allow 3 weeks for delivery.